DEER TALK

DEER TALK

Your Guide to Finding, Calling, and Hunting
Mule Deer and Whitetails, with Rifle, Bow or Camera

By Don Laubach and Mark Henckel

Library of Congress Catalog Card Number 92-72270
ISBN 1-931832-46-3

Published by:
Don Laubach
Box 85
Gardiner, MT 59030

Distributed by:
Riverbend Publishing
PO Box 5833
Helena, MT 59604
toll-free (866) 787-2363

Cover and illustrations by John Potter

Printed in the United States of America.

Dedication

This book is dedicated
to mule deer, whitetails and blacktails
that these magnificent animals
may always roam
the wild places of North America

TABLE OF CONTENTS

ACKNOWLEDGMENTS

Nobody does anything on his own. We all rely on the people who came before us. That seems to be especially true of deer hunting. Some person invented the gun or devised the bow. Somebody else loaded the ammunition or manufactured the arrow. The biologists and game wardens protected our deer herds. The camera makers were inspired to create cameras and film to capture moments in time. And our ancestors provided us with a heritage of hunting to provide meat for our tables and set aside places for wild deer to roam. The list could go on and on.

So if this is a pioneering book on deer calling, understand first and foremost that all we're really doing here is taking the many things that have been learned by those who came before us and adding a few more pieces to the puzzle that is deer hunting. Even those few new pieces were not created by us alone. There are people who richly deserve much of the credit.

Wildlife filmmaker Gordon Eastman has been more than just a good friend. His dedication to and understanding of the outdoors and the wildlife that lives there has been a constant inspiration without which the Deer Talk call would never have been developed and the language of deer would never have been understood. The memories of calling deer he has captured on film are images that will never fade.

Thanks to Don Snyder, Jerry Gillum, Dick Hosford, Billy Hoppe, Russ Condra, Mike Schwiebert, Mike Murphy and Murphy Love for their feedback on the calls.

Many thanks, too, to Wade Laubach for his help with experimentation and development of the call and to Kirk and Ryan Laubach for building the calls.

There are debts of gratitude to wildlife biologists like Dick Mackie, Ken Hamlin, Dave Pac, Helga Ihsle-Pac, Gary Dusek, Charlie Eustace, Shawn Stewart, Claire Simmons, Harold Wentland, Neil Martin, Bernie Hildebrand, Shawn Riley, Arnold Dood, Heidi Youmans, John Cada, Graham Taylor, Terry Lonner and Phil Schladweiler for providing background on the habits and lifestyles of deer. Over the years, they've been asked countless questions and always managed to answer them with explanations that even I could understand.

Artist John Potter graced the pages of the book with his fine drawings of mule and white-tailed deer. Wildlife photographers Michael H. Francis, Jim Hamilton, Frank R. Martin, and Bob Zellar allowed us to raid their files and show you their fine talents with a camera.

Finally, there are proofreaders like Dee Laubach, Colleen Crawford and Carol Henckel. They haven't laughed too hard at the typos or garbled grammar and have always offered inspiration and support when needed the most.

To our families, thank you for the time it took away from the things we could have been doing with you.

To our other commitments, thank you for allowing us to steal the time to write about something we really enjoy.

To our children—Wade, Kirk, Ryan and Lori in Gardiner and Andy and Matt in Park City—and all our hunting partners over the years, thank you for allowing us to tell tales about all the good times we've spent together.

Without the efforts and indulgence of all of these people, *Deer Talk* never would have rolled off the presses.

FOREWORD

Life is never easy for the pioneer. Just as our forefathers had to stand alone in the forests, on the prairie and high in the mountains in the face of fires, pestilence and the whims of nature, we're standing alone here in the face of deer hunting tradition and experts on all sides. And frankly, it's a little scary.

Deer that talk? Making deer talk? Calling in deer in all seasons? It sounds sort of strange. It's certainly new. And it's decidedly radical. In fact, it flies in the face of almost every piece of expert advice that hunters have grown up with.

Yet that's exactly what this book is all about. It's not rattling in bucks and making grunt calls. It's the basic language that both mule deer and whitetails learn when they're fawns. It's calling in a buck in the middle of an open field in the middle of the day. It's stopping a deer that's running away at full speed and making that deer turn around and look at you.

Even experienced deer hunters are going to raise an eyebrow at claims like that. All we can say is that we're pioneering new ground in our dealings with deer here. We're asking you to keep an open mind. We're hoping you give it a try and find the same success that we've had with deer talk.

In the pages that follow, you'll read about the theories we've come up with regarding deer communication. You'll read about the Deer Talk call and such new terminology as common doe sounds, half-distress sounds and distress sounds. In the two fall seasons since the first prototypes of Deer Talk were put in hunters' hands, we've had some exciting experiences ourselves with those sounds and have heard about some amazing experiences of others. We'll share those stories with you throughout the text of *Deer Talk*.

Hopefully, you'll come away from this book with something new and different to try on your deer hunting or photography trips. Hopefully, you'll add to the body of knowledge and explore some new frontiers yourself. Whether you buy and use the Deer Talk call or find another way to make the proper sounds, this book will give you a starting point. Believe me, the world of communication with whitetails and mule deer is far from being totally conquered.

Before you begin your pioneering and read any further in this book, there are a few ground rules we'd like to point out that served us well when we wrote our two previous collaborations, *Elk Talk* and *The Elk Hunter*. You'll probably notice, for example, that after using the word "hunter" in the first reference, we'll probably follow with pronouns like "he," "his" and "him." That's not meant to be a slight against any women who happen to be reading the book. But efforts to de-sex the book by calling them "outdoorpersons," "outdoorpeoplepersons," "unisexgunners" or even "hunter-humans" just didn't work out. Don figured that he'd get his tongue twisted too badly out of shape when he tried to say them into the microphone of his tape recorder. Mark knew he'd never spell them write when it came to righting the book.

Another similarity between this book and the previous two will be to use the universal "I" when referring to the experiences of either of us. Once again, it makes the book easier to read and understand than trying to explain about how Don did this or Mark did that. And using the name "Don-Mark" was just too unwieldy.

For that reason, Don is "I" and Mark is "I." Anyone who's called "my good friend" or "my partner" is just a friend or partner of one of us that the other hasn't met yet. As for the term "my son," that also is a two-family affair.

With all those semantics behind, we hope you enjoy *Deer Talk*. It's presented to you in a down-to-earth style that's been written for the lay hunter and outdoorsman. You won't find many biological terms and scientific definitions simply because we're not biologists or scientists.

We're just hunters and outdoorsmen, just like you. But we're going to tell you some exciting news about talking to whitetails and mule deer. We're going to break new ground in terms of deer communication. And hopefully, as you turn the pages of *Deer Talk*, we're going to turn you into pioneers, too.

So sit back, keep an open mind and enjoy. You're going to take a radical journey into the wild world of Deer Talk.

Don Laubach
Gardiner, Montana

Mark Henckel
Park City, Montana

DEER TALK

Deer Do Talk

I've heard it too many times before—and I hear it yet today—deer don't talk. Bucks might grunt during the rut. Does might snort at danger. Fawns might squeal when a predator has them. But as far as any kind of real language is concerned, deer just don't have one. They don't, anyway, have a language that a person can rely on as far as calling to them and expecting them to respond to your call anytime you want in any season of the year.

It's been written that way in the popular hunting press. It's been presented in seminars by people who call themselves deer hunting experts. Over the years, it has been told and retold so often that almost everyone has come to believe it as the gospel truth.

I'm here to tell you, however, that nothing could be further from the truth. Deer do talk to each other. Other deer listen. You can call them in by making the proper sounds. And you can do a lot of other things when you speak their language, too. You can, for example, stop a fleeing buck

When you can really call well, you can lure deer right to your window. Don Laubach photo.

dead in his tracks. You can cause deer to get up out of their beds and move around or band together with other deer. You can lull deer into a state of calm when they're distressed. You can talk to bucks, does and fawns with a call. In fact, anyone can.

These are some radical statements, I know. It's almost blasphemous when compared to the gospel we've all been taught about deer over the years. It's magical, mystical and, to be frank, quite a mouthful that would be awfully hard to prove if there wasn't a growing body of evidence to strongly back it up.

To start with, let me explain that this deer language that we're talking about isn't limited to any deer species or any particular part of the country. It has worked on whitetails, mule deer and blacktails. I've heard reports of success from the East, West and places in between. And those reports have come from rifle hunters, bowhunters and wildlife photographers. Perhaps the best thing about it is the speed with which those reports have come.

After all, deer talk could be called the new frontier. Although its basis has been around for decades, and hunters have sporadically made the sounds, its understanding and widespread use is a relatively recent phenomenon. But it's spreading, and spreading fast.

The best way to illustrate that spread is to tell you a story related to me by a Wyoming outfitter. It all started with a hunter in California who bought elk calls from me in the past and purchased one of my Deer Talk calls last summer. His first day out with the call, he called in twenty-five blacktails, eleven of them bucks. Shortly before the archery season started there, he bought a bow and practiced with it and called in a nice blacktail buck that he shot at twenty-two yards.

That fall, the California hunter and a friend traveled to Wyoming to hunt with the outfitter. On opening day, they jumped twelve mule deer bucks in a canyon. Those bucks lined out at a dead run for a patch of distant timber. The outfitter told the hunter that they'd have to get moving to head off those bucks before they disappeared. But the California hunter told him that he'd like to try the call first. When he blew it, all twelve bucks stopped dead in their tracks and the hunter aimed his rifle and shot a fine buck with a thirty-inch spread. At that, the outfitter understandably said, "Holy smokes, what have you got there?" Later in the hunt, the California hunter and his partner used archery gear and the call to fill mule deer doe permits with shots of ten yards and twelve yards.

Not surprisingly, after the California hunters left, the outfitter got hold of me and ordered a bunch of deer calls. One of those calls found its way back East with one of the outfitter's clients, after a successful hunt in Wyoming. The hunter who took it, a grandfather, passed the call along to his grandson and told him to use it while he was archery hunting for whitetails. The boy went out on his grandfather's farm, climbed a tree, and was still sitting up there at about ten in the morning when he decided to call it quits. When the boy came down, he spooked a doe that he hadn't seen. So he decided to use the call. When the doe came back

A deer call will work as well on big muley bucks as on does and fawns.
Michael H. Francis photo.

to the call, she brought a six-point, eastern count, whitetail buck with her. The boy dropped the buck with a single arrow to the spine. He dropped the bow, ran back to the farmhouse, and spread the happy news of his success to his grandfather, who told the Wyoming outfitter, who told me.

California to Wyoming to Wisconsin—success all around on blacktails, mule deer and whitetails. It sounds too good

Templeton Wells used a deer call to take a buck with Russ Condra.
Templeton Wells photo.

to be true, even to me and I know it's true. I also know that the successes these hunters found with the call aren't isolated incidents. They're being repeated by others along with a lot of other wild things that just a few years ago I wouldn't have dreamed would be possible.

To me, as the manufacturer of the Deer Talk call, it's gratifying to hear the stories. It's always nice to know that someone who bought your product found some success with it. To be honest, it's the fondest dream of anyone who produces a game call or anything else that it fills the buyers' needs and brings them happiness. Those are the kinds of stories that I never get tired of reading about in letters.

But it's not the purpose of this book. While I can tell you that the Deer Talk call makes the right sounds to communicate with deer, there are undoubtedly other ways to make them, too. I was making some of the noises—and finding spasmodic success with them—almost four decades ago with such varied methods as blowing predator calls and blades of grass pressed between my thumbs.

What this book is about is the store of knowledge that's

being developed on calling in deer. It's going to tell you about the deer themselves and their communication. It's going to tell you how to communicate with them. It's going to tell you where to look for deer and how to find them. It's going to go over some old ground about deer and break new ground about calling.

Whether you buy a Deer Talk call or not, the aim of *Deer Talk*, the book, is to help you gain a new appreciation for mule deer, whitetails and blacktails alike. It's going to pull together some of the loose ends for experienced hunters and explain the phenomena that they've witnessed in the field, but may not have understood. It's going to give the novice hunter a leg up in the sport. And for those who simply enjoy watching wild deer and perhaps taking a photograph or some video footage of them, it's going to give them an exciting new tool to make their time in the outdoors far more enjoyable.

If it sounds like I'm excited about deer talk, rest assured that I am. Like you, the reader of this book, I'm still learning about it every time I head toward the deer woods, the mountains or the prairie and pull out my call. But I'll share with you what I've learned already and tell you some tales from the past and recount the things others have told me about what they've done.

The world of deer talk is an exciting new frontier. If you really love deer like I do, come along with me and we'll explore it together in the pages ahead.

FAWN TALK

They All Say It

Trying to understand and imitate the language of animals is certainly nothing new. I'm sure somewhere in the deep, dark past, there was an American Indian who heard a bull elk bugle, told himself, "Hey, I can make that noise," and promptly produced a pretty good bugle. I can only imagine that Indian's surprise when the bull elk responded, charged to within feet of him, raked his broad antlers on the ground, roared another bugle right in his ear and looked all around for the other bull, just spoiling for a fight. It must have been a real eye-opener for that early-day hunter. And he must have said something to himself like, "Wow! Wait 'til the guys back at camp hear about this one!"

You can go through a litany of other wildlife species that also were imitated and found to respond to a call. Wild turkeys, for example, have a whole repertoire of sounds that they make which hunters repeat. A good duck caller can sound like an entire flock of ducks and the sounds that he makes will represent everything from feeding calls to gathering calls to calls of contentment. Predator hunters will imitate wounded rabbits to lure foxes and coyotes within rifle range. And elk hunters have recently undergone a big revolution of their own, expanding on the old bull bugles to include sounds of cows and calves into their calling sequences.

So why not call in deer? The question isn't a new one. In fact, it was a question I asked myself when I was still a young hunter back in the 1950s. There was some basis for my wondering.

Hunters in the West have long known that mule deer sometimes come in to predator calls. Why? They didn't really know. But almost everyone who has spent much time out calling for coyotes has stories to tell about how does have come in to the sounds. So why not me, too?

In 1955, I began using a predator call during deer hunting season. Sometimes, does came in. Other times, it sent them screaming away like rockets. Why? I didn't know. I did know it worked some of the time. So did taking a blade of grass between your two thumbs and blowing through it to create a flat humming sound. But there was nothing consistent about the results. There was no sense of assuredness that the calling would work.

To be honest with you, I just tucked the knowledge away for the next thirty years or so. It was a freak, a novelty. It was one of those miscellaneous pieces of woods lore that you pick up along the way when you spend days and weeks and seasons out in the field. That was one reason I didn't pursue it. The other was that it wasn't really necessary. You could take your deer in other ways in Montana and rare was the season when I really wanted one that my tag wasn't filled.

Why hasn't someone else gone beyond the grunt calls used during the rut and the bleat call used to imitate fawns? That's simple. They were sure that deer didn't really rely on their voices for communication the way so many other species did.

Let's face it, when a bull elk uses his voice during the rut, you know it. Even a half-deaf elk hunter can hear that high-pitched whistle for a mile or more as it cuts through the still mountain air.

When you visit a marsh full of ducks and geese, you can hear their chatter just as easily. Spend as much time in a duck blind as some hunters and guides have and you're bound to pick out the various sounds that they make.

The same thing is true of turkeys. Toms will gobble. Hens will yelp and cluck and putt. Put a zillion hunters out in the woods every year with a box call or slate call in their hands and they're bound to learn real quick which sounds to make and which sounds to avoid at all costs.

But deer have always been different. You very rarely hear them make any noise at all. But the noise is there, if you're close enough to hear it. If you've got the aid of a shotgun microphone, you can hear it even better. In fact, you'll hear a lot of different sounds come out of deer, just as the vocabulary of elk is far more varied than most hunters would ever believe.

I know now that thirty years ago, when I was experimenting with the predator call, what I was really imitating was the distress call of a fawn. It's the same sound that most practitioners of the bleat call rely on to lure in deer.

But I know now, too, that the distress call of a fawn is a touchy sound indeed. It brings in does—sometimes. It works best on the lead doe of a group—if you can fool her. And the only way it can work on a buck is if that buck happens to trail in after the doe or happens to be running away and stops to get a better listen to the distress call.

My newfound curiosity that there must be other sounds that a deer makes actually began in 1986 when I developed the Cow Talk elk call. The call worked on elk, certainly. But deer seemed to react to it, too. Not all the time, maybe. But certainly some of the time. And the way they reacted to it was different than with distress sounds. With the Cow Talk call, I could get deer to stop and investigate and even come closer. Instead of being edgy, the call seemed to calm them down, just as it did the elk.

There must have been something in the elk call. There had to be a sound in there that struck a chord with the mule

Fawn Talk ■

deer that co-inhabited the elk range. It was certainly worth exploring further.

Over the past few years, I've set to work tinkering with that elk call, altering the sounds and watching the reaction of the mule deer in our area to the changes I made. Living in a mule deer-rich area, I had plenty of subjects to work on. During the winter months, thousands of deer pour out of the high country in and around Yellowstone National Park to spend the cold months in the lowlands and valleys. To me, it was the perfect laboratory for experimentation. There were plenty of deer. And there were plenty of deer you could get close to. What I set out to do was to make the most of the situation and come up with a mule deer call— just a mule deer call.

As time went by and I spent more time with the deer, I got close enough to hear the flat little call that they make. When I imitated the noise back to them, they'd make the call again.

While filming video footage with the Cody, Wyoming, cinematographer Gordon Eastman, we had the opportunity to use shotgun microphones to augment our own hearing. Imagine our surprise when we took footage of mule deer that we were sure were silent during our filming, only to run it through a television and find out with the amplified sounds that the deer were actually talking back to us and communicating with each other all the while.

What we learned was that the common language among deer is a soft one. It isn't very loud at all. If you're more than about twenty yards away and not listening for it, you might not hear it at all. It's a low sound. It's a flat sound. Yet that single, monotone note that takes no more than a second or two to make, was the magic I'd begun looking for when I blew on that predator call thirty years earlier.

As we experimented with what would become the Deer Talk call, we began perfecting the sound. We did it in much the same way as elk hunters, turkey hunters and duck hunters did it years and years ago. We listened to the deer and imitated what we heard.

Our experimentation with deer sounds led to the Deer Talk call.
Don Laubach photo.

The story that perhaps best illustrates the scope of our natural workshop and how we used it involved my son Wade when he had one of the early prototypes. Wade, who lives toward the edge of Gardiner, was working in his backyard and noticed several deer on the hillside not too far behind his house. So he got his call and began talking to them. And the deer responded, coming right into his yard.

Fawn Talk ■

As Wade made his deer sounds, the size of his backyard herd began to grow until it reached twenty-one animals, some of them literally around the porch he was sitting on. Wade called to them. They answered him back. All the while, Wade kept adjusting the rubber band that served as the reed on his call, trying to exactly imitate the sounds that the deer themselves were making. By the time he was done, some deer were standing within five feet of him.

That backyard exhibition certainly made a believer out of Wade. In the midst of his telling me about it, he also passed the news along that the deer weren't all making the same exact sounds. And the sound we had been making was just a little off, too. So he picked out the most common sound that he heard and that was the one he used to tune his call.

The sound that Wade heard, the one that Gordon and I heard the most, and the sound that has proven to be the most versatile in talking to deer is something we dubbed the common doe sound. It's a name that stuck and one we're still using today to describe that short, flat, monotone sound that forms the basis for deer talk.

As I said, we set out to develop a call for mule deer. In those first years of prototypes, that's just what we did. What we didn't realize at the time, however, was that the sounds we were making were not limited to mule deer alone. At least, the responses we've been getting from whitetail hunters and blacktail hunters tell us that the language is not limited to mule deer alone.

To be truthful, all we can figure is that the voice structures within the throats of all deer must be pretty much the same. That's how we explain it. All we know for sure is that it works great here and we've heard enough responses from hunters all over the country that it works great elsewhere, too.

As for the contention that deer don't talk except at certain times of the year, that's not true at all. I've heard them too many times in too many seasons. They just talk softly, that's all. You have to listen real close to hear them. And you have to read on to know how to respond.

Deer communicate with each other in many ways including touch.
Jim Hamilton photo.

Early Life

Life must come as quite a shock for the fawns of the world. Imagine going from the warmth and security of a doe's womb to a tough landing on the hard earth. Imagine the blinding sun, sweltering temperatures, drenching rains, thunder and lightning, hailstorms, swarms of mosquitoes and the biting flies and ticks. Depending on where they're born and the whims of the weather, newborn fawns could face any or all of these things. Those first weeks of life must be a rude awakening indeed.

Yet somehow, against the odds, most fawns survive. Though they're only six to nine pounds at birth and look to be all legs, these children of the wild are tough little critters. They have to be. They're so small and frail. A wide variety of predators including coyotes, bears, eagles, mountain lions and even foxes are out to make a meal of them. They're new and inexperienced and trying to learn. But, of course, they've got their mothers to help them along.

The bonding of does and fawns comes almost instantly. As soon as the fawns are dropped, their mothers lick them clean. As soon as they can get on their feet, they begin to nurse. That's the way life always begins, a bonding of mother and newborn that will be critical to the survival of the fawn.

Most often, the doe will have two fawns to care for that way. That's the norm for does in good condition. If the doe's condition is poor going into winter or if the stresses of winter are severe, there may only be one fawn. If the doe's condition is excellent and nature smiles on her, there could be triplets or even quadruplets. But two fawns are the usual delivery in the weeks of late May and early June. And, frankly, two fawns are enough for any deer mother to handle.

When you encounter even newborn fawns, you can't help but be amazed at the instincts these animals are born with. From the start, they know that their best defense is to lie perfectly still and hope that predators don't see them.

On several occasions, I've been along with wildlife biologists who have caught young fawns to fit them with radio collars. Each time, the younger the fawn, the more likely it was to stay in cover and hold there motionless while the biologists moved in with long-handled nets. And you'd be surprised how tough the fawns were to spot, even when you were within a few feet of them. The older the fawn, the more likely it was to scramble to its feet and run before you

Young fawns are often left alone while the doe moves off to feed.
Jim Hamilton photo.

got within netting range. But young or old, their spotted coats provided them with excellent camouflage.

Lying motionless and relatively scentless, the fawns quickly grow used to being alone. In fact, leaving the fawns alone seems to be one of the defense mechanisms that all members of the deer family use. The doe will return only for feeding and nurturing, then leave the fawn alone for hours at a time while the doe wanders away to feed on her own. In some cases, in open country, the doe could wander a mile away.

Fawn Talk ■

This tendency for the does and fawns to be separated during the early weeks of a fawn's life is one reason why so many people think fawns have been abandoned when they find them lying alone. The truth is that relatively few fawns are ever abandoned, and those that are left are more likely to have had a young and inexperienced doe as a mother. Old does are extremely reliable in caring for and protecting their young. Besides, just the fact that someone finds a living fawn is generally proof that the fawn is being cared for. With the heavy nutritional needs of a fawn, it would die quickly if the doe wasn't providing for it.

While the doe does, indeed, spend a great deal of time away from her fawns, there is a great deal of love and nurturing shown by these deer mothers when they are around their young. All it takes is some time spent watching a doe and fawn together to realize that there is communication between the two. Some of that communication is done by body movements and nuzzling. Does will lick their young to clean them and show affection. The fawn will learn body language—like the erect posture of a whitetail's tail or the ears being alert on a mule deer—to show danger may be nearby. And, certainly, some of the communication is done vocally.

How quickly the fawn learns vocalizations from its mother is a matter of conjecture. When you consider that does typically move away from their previous year's fawns and seek secluded spots to drop their new ones, it isn't surprising that people are rarely around to see fawns being born. Wildlife filmmaker Gordon Eastman did get one inkling of how early the fawns learn vocalization while he was filming whitetails in a Pennsylvania deer enclosure.

A doe within the enclosure had dropped twin fawns within hours of when he began filming. They were barely able to get up on their spindly legs and walk. As Gordon filmed the pair, he pulled out a deer call and began making soft, short fawn calls. When the fawn heard the sounds, it immediately walked over to him and laid down, curling up right between his legs.

All you can gather from the fawn's reactions was that it had heard those sounds before in the few hours since its birth. Why else would the fawn have come to the sound and acted the way it did?

Equally interesting was the fact that the doe didn't respond to the sound. In fact, the doe seemed to ignore it. Yet when Gordon changed the pitch of his calling and made some distress sounds, he got her attention immediately. That distress call was something that she, as a mother, was programmed to respond to. But she wasn't going to be called over by the natural noises of a newborn fawn.

It should be noted also that in addition to getting the doe's attention with the distress call, Gordon also caught the attention of a whitetail buck still in the velvet.

You can draw your own conclusions as to why the deer were and weren't responding. All I could figure was that during fawning time, the distress call meant that a newborn was in trouble. During that time, it wasn't just one fawn's mother that was responding, but all adults in the area. The other conclusion that I drew was that fawns making their soft noises aren't all that uncommon. It's not uncommon enough, anyway, that the deer are going to come over to the fawn just because it's making a little noise.

Adding more ammunition to the argument that fawns use their voices and does are attuned to them are the experiences of Montana wildlife photographer Michael H. Francis. Francis also used one of the prototypes of the Deer Talk call while he was shooting photographs for the fine book *Mule Deer Country* which he collaborated on with Dr. Valerius Geist for NorthWord Press.

Francis had taken thousands of deer photographs over the years, but needed more photos of fawns in order to complete the work. The deer call helped him. He said that when he blew the call, the does would pick up their heads and look directly at where the fawn was lying. They wouldn't go over to the spot. But all he had to do was follow the line of their vision and he knew where to search to locate the fawn so he could take the photographs he needed.

Fawn Talk

Deer learn to communicate with sound very early in their lives.
Jim Hamilton photo.

Why did the does look that way and not go over to where the fawn was for Francis? I don't really know. We can speculate that they heard the call Francis was making and just wanted to make sure it wasn't their own fawn calling. All we can say is that they heard the call and responded.

While we may not know the reasons or be able to explain the language and exactly what we're saying to the deer, we do know that they respond to the calls. They have responded so many times in so many different ways that the theory of deer vocalization we're developing with common doe sounds and fawn sounds and distress calls has to have some basis. That basis, we believe, is in the vocalization of deer early in their lives, fawn-to-doe and doe-to-fawn.

It's something they learn early and that sticks with them for the rest of their lives. Their voices may change when they get older, just as people's voices change. They may learn new sounds to add to their repertoire, just as people learn new things to say and new ways to say them. But the principle is the same.

Just as people can't seem to ignore the sound of a crying baby, adult deer can't ignore the sound of a fawn in distress. Just as an adult human can tune out the sounds of babbling children, adult deer can tune out the normal vocalizations of a fawn. And just as you'd check on your own child to make sure it was still safe and secure when another mother was calling somewhere else, the deer react in the same way.

That's the theory anyway which we've developed from the evidence that the fawns are providing us. In the months and years to come, hopefully we'll be able to add to our knowledge and be able to tell you more about it. But I can tell you now that from what we've seen already, we're excited by the possibilities.

All we can tell you now for sure is that the reactions we've gotten from the deer have already helped to take better photographs and get a closer look at some of nature's most beautiful newborns just by making deer talk during fawning time.

Fawn Talk ■

Does and Bucks

Deer are pretty much the same. And yet, they're all different. It all comes down to whether you're a lumper or a splitter.

Zoologists are the ones who look at animals and decide whether they're the same or different. Lumpers are the ones who tend to lump animals together and say they're members of the same species or subspecies. Splitters are the ones who tend to create more species or subspecies. Scientifically, it's always a battle with one side winning some of the fights and the other side winning some.

The textbooks tell us that the current standing in the battle for deer is that there are seventeen subspecies of whitetailed deer and eight subspecies of mule deer. The whitetails range from the Northwest, Dakota and Northern Woodland to some that are found only on specific islands off the Atlantic Coast. For the mule deer, there are subspecies ranging from the Rocky Mountain and Desert to the Sitka Blacktail and the Columbia Blacktail.

Whether you're a lumper or a splitter, all agree that the general trend of deer is that those in climes further north tend to be larger in body size. Those further south tend to have smaller bodies. For whitetails or mule deer, the trend is the same.

Also, although the two species and their many subspecies may have their differences, it is unmistakable when you see them that all are deer. Their basic body structures are the same. Their internal working mechanisms are basically the same. And, in large measure, the way they live their lives are the same.

Any doe of any subspecies, for example, is an old, old deer when it reaches the age of twelve. The bucks will be very old if they live past the age of seven. Healthy does will drop twin fawns each spring. Healthy bucks will shed their antlers in early winter. Bucks and does will be in the rut anywhere from the last week of October to the first week of December.

Bucks will hang together in groups throughout much of the year.
Bob Zellar photo.

The biggest differences between the bucks and does, aside from the obvious sexual characteristics, will be in their lifestyles. Bucks and does actually live separate lives for most of the year. The reason all comes down to the survival of the species and the way that survival has evolved over time.

Because of the importance of the does in reproduction and the demands of carrying, delivering and nurturing fawns, they live a more energy-conserving lifestyle and tend to make more use and better use of available range. They need to build extensive fat reserves over the course of the summer and hold onto them through the fall because the fawns they'll be carrying over the winter will demand everything the does can offer. It's also true that older does, who have dropped fawns before, tend to be better mothers. Hence, there is a premium for the species on having does survive to older ages.

Fawn Talk ■

Bucks on the other hand, and I almost hate to say it, are more expendable. The only time of year they're really necessary to the species is during the breeding season. While does will select the larger, healthier bucks for breeding, they can be bred successfully even by younger animals. And buck numbers aren't that critical. One buck can service many does. As a result, nature doesn't really care that mortality rates among bucks tend to be higher and that bucks tend to die younger.

Nature provides for some of the increased mortality among bucks by having a birthing ratio that slightly favors bucks. Statistically, more bucks than does are born. But because of the more tenacious nature of the males, more bucks tend to die of accidental deaths. Because they run off their fat reserves chasing does that may or may not be responsive to their overtures in fall, they enter winter in a run-down condition and are an easy mark for winter kill. And because the older they get, the more active they tend to be in the breeding, the less likely it becomes with each passing year that they'll survive to see spring.

It should be pointed out, too, that deer tend to live in a matriarchal society. The oldest vital mom tends to be the leader, especially among mule deer. Mule deer tend to be more herd-oriented all year long than whitetails and tend to live in wide-open places so you can see their association. For that reason, the matriarchal nature of their society shows up more graphically to the casual observer.

When you a see a group of mule deer does and fawns together, it's a pretty good bet that they're related. If a mature buck is with them, it's a pretty good bet that the buck isn't.

While mule deer does will separate from the previous year's fawns to drop new ones, they will often reunite with those old fawns, especially if they are does. Doe groups will build that way to the point that there could be grandmothers, aunts, daughters, nieces and granddaughters within a herd group.

Bucks tend to disperse to new areas when they reach one-

and-a-half or two-and-a-half years old. The doe groups they tend to associate with will be the products of unrelated mothers. Logic would tell you that the success of this method of dispersal would protect against inbreeding among deer.

As fawns get big enough to move around with their mothers, you'll often see groups of mule deer does and fawns together during the weeks of late summer and fall. These doe groups may have a young buck with them or they may not.

While the does are busy with their young fawns, mature bucks may also gather in groups. It's not uncommon to see two or more mule deer bucks hanging together. One time, I saw a herd of twenty-one bucks in a group, all of them good bucks, but groups that large are relatively rare.

These bachelor herds will often hang together during summer and early fall. I'm sure that just as the older does teach the younger does and fawns about their way of life, the older bucks pass on the traditions of their particular herd to the younger bucks. As antlers harden in preparation for the rut, there is also considerable good-natured sparring that goes on among the deer of the bachelor herds. As much as anything, this heads off confrontations later on when the rut gets in full swing. By that time, either the sparring partners have met before or they at least know their capabilities and who they dare tackle. As a result, the only actual battles of the rut will be between two bucks of about the same size.

As I said before, the only true mixing of all bucks and all does will come during the rut for mule deer and perhaps again on the winter range. During the months of spring, summer and early fall, the bucks and does basically live their separate lives.

The fact that winter comes so close on the heels of the rut may explain how bucks find the winter range. With the breeding time roughly coinciding with the time that does are heading toward winter range, younger bucks might find their way there by scent alone. Older bucks, certainly, will remember where the winter ranges are.

Whitetail characteristics are basically the same, but they

The rut in autumn will bring does and bucks to the same area.
Frank R. Martin photo.

can be much harder to distinguish, especially in the East, because so much of their lives may be spent in the relatively close confines of hardwood forests.

Like mule deer, whitetails, too, tend to form matriarchal groups of related does and fawns in the fall. Like mule deer, it's the older does that pass on the traditions of survival by leading the way toward yarding areas where the winter will be spent. And, again like mule deer, the whitetail bucks are basically treated as expendable by nature once the rut is done. They, too, tend to gather in the deer yards with the does, but winter will be tough on them with few fat reserves to help them through.

The thing to remember about bucks and does and the differences between them is that nature has dictated a strategy of survival for the species or subspecies, not the individual. The lifestyles that deer follow are the ones that have kept the species alive over the centuries. If some deer were lost along the way, it was because their strategy of survival didn't work out over time.

So while one hunter may be talking about whitetails and another might be talking about mule deer, remember that although they can be different in many respects, there are also many ways in which they're the same. When talking about calling in deer, it's the sameness that surprised us the most. We never figured that talking to mule deer does and bucks would be much the same as talking to whitetail does and bucks. But it has turned out to be very much the same.

While the lumpers and splitters have dictated the species and many subspecies of mule deer and whitetails, nature seems to have provided them with a voice box that's pretty much the same.

DOE TALK

Universal Language

Believe it or not, deer speak a universal language, whether they're fawns, bucks or does. They might speak it a little differently. Fawns talk a bit higher and shorter. Does and bucks talk a little lower and longer. But the language is really all the same.

Why it took me so many years to discover this is a mystery even to me. After all, elk are members of the deer family. And that's just the way their language works. Elk were just a lot easier to figure out.

For one thing, elk talk a lot louder than deer. When you're hunting the wild places of fall, you can hear them talking easily when there are elk around. The bugles of the bulls echo through the mountains of September and early October in Montana. Cows barking their warning calls can be heard for several hundred yards. The chirping of calves as they walk or play are easily heard at least half that far away.

It wasn't hard to hear that elk language and we imitated it effectively with diaphragm turkey calls or grunt tubes when we were hunting twenty years ago. At the time, however, we were stuck on the bugling bulls and the fact that by bugling back at them, we could entice them to come in for a fight. It worked well enough during the rut. We took our share of bulls. And the cow and calf sounds we heard were passed off as just novelty sounds. After all, we weren't really hunting for cows and calves so why should we imitate them?

It wasn't until the last decade that I figured out that making the cow and calf sounds would bring in the bulls, too. The calves made a higher-pitched, shorter sound. The cows made a deeper, longer sound. But every elk in the mountains would respond to the calls. So I built my Cow Talk call and have been happily hunting elk with it ever since. Looking back, it was so simple I could kick myself for not having thought of it sooner.

The truth about learning hunting skills, however, is that all things don't come as easily as pointing a rifle and pulling the trigger. When learning about the animals themselves, it takes time to observe the animals. It takes many observations. You do some reading about the animals. You talk to other hunters. Finally, you begin to pick up patterns that give you an insight into what's going on. I like to compare it to a giant puzzle. Each time you hunt or talk or read, you pick up pieces. As the pieces begin to pile up, you begin to find out that they fit together. But the truth of the matter is that it takes many, many pieces and many, many years of putting them together before the picture takes shape of what you're actually witnessing in the outdoors.

That's one of the reasons it took so long to learn about the universal language of deer. In looking back at it, I picked up pieces back in the 1950s with the predator call. I picked up more as I read and heard about and tried the grunt calls and bleat calls. But probably the biggest breakthrough in putting the puzzle together came when I learned about the language of elk. After all, if the elk are talking a common language, why not deer which are members of the same family?

It should have been logical, too, that with deer being smaller than elk, their language wouldn't be as loud. But who could have imagined how soft it was? And who would have imagined that making soft calls yourself would be the most effective?

Once again, the pieces of the puzzle fell together. As I said earlier, the use of a shotgun microphone helped. It amplified sounds that I didn't realize they were making, even when I was talking to deer and they were talking back. What I found was that unless you are within about forty yards of them, you don't hear them, even on a calm, quiet day. At that distance, you still have to listen closely, because the noise they make isn't loud.

Billy Hoppe, an outfitter friend of mine who lives outside of Gardiner, has heard them talking when they come into his ranch yard to clean up hay left behind by his horses. At those times, he's within twenty to thirty feet of them and he can hear their low noises quite plainly. During the winter, he always has quite a crew of deer that move in. But from what Billy tells me, just having the deer there isn't a sure thing, either. Sometimes they chatter a lot. Other times, they feed silently. He doesn't know why there's a difference between the days. Neither do I.

It is logical, however, that deer wouldn't need to talk loud to be heard. If you consider the size of their ears, especially on the mule deer, you have a sound-gathering system that would put even the shotgun mike to shame.

From my experimenting with my own call over the past few years, I can tell you that mule deer can pick up a soft call from about 500 yards away if the day is quiet and the calling is done in open country. Other experimenting has shown me that the same sound the mule deer are picking up at 500 yards, a human can't even hear at seventy-five yards. It doesn't take much deduction to realize that our calling theories are all wrong when applied to the animals we're calling. We've always been using our own ears and hearing abilities to determine how loud we're blowing our calls. What we should be doing is considering the strength of the

Deer can use their ears like radar to detect sounds far away.
Jim Hamilton photo.

senses of the animals themselves. For deer anyway, when applied to the old bleat calls, they must have figured we were shouting at them. Is it any wonder the sound wasn't exactly right to lure them in on a consistent basis?

While mule deer can hear the soft calls that far away, whitetails' hearing wouldn't be quite as sensitive simply because of the terrain in which they're found. Trees and brush would tend to soak up the sound and deflect it. As a result, the hearing range of whitetails would be much shorter.

The rule of thumb I've developed for myself is that I figure a deer can probably hear five or six times as well as I can. With that as my guide and keeping in mind that blow-

Because of terrain, whitetails may not hear calls from a long distance.
Frank R. Martin photo.

ing the call softly is better than blowing it too loud, I try to
make my sounds as soft as I can.

The other thing to realize about both your calling and the
deer talk itself is that weather conditions can change sounds
a great deal.

There is no other enemy that looms as large to the hunter
with a call as the wind. If the wind is light, you might be
able to use it to carry a sound in the direction of the deer, if
you happen to be exactly upwind. But any wind stronger
than a light wind will almost surely doom you to failure.

For one thing, wind seems to distort the sounds. It does
with sounds as loud as an elk makes. I'm sure it does the
same with the sounds of a deer. The deer's ability to hear is
also affected by it. Just as the sounds heard through a shotgun mike will deteriorate into nothing more than the hiss of
the blowing wind, I'm sure the deer can't hear in strong

Doe Talk

winds either. If you doubt that, just watch them the next time you see them when the wind is blowing hard. The deer are skittish. They're more apt to run. They won't stick around to pinpoint the danger before heading out. They just head out. I'm convinced it's because with the loss of their hearing to the wind, they don't feel as safe and secure.

I'm not going to tell you that I've figured out all the pieces of the calling puzzle. Far from it. I've figured out some of them over the past few years. I haven't put them all together.

But just as my elk calling effectiveness improved with the use of a cow call, my deer hunting has been more effective since I started using a deer call. As the years pass, I'm sure I'll get even better with the cow call. I'm sure I'll get better with the deer call, too.

Why write a book about something that I haven't totally figured out yet? For one thing, to spread the word. For another, because the things you learn about the call will increase the knowledge we all have about the language of deer and how it fits into their lives.

As I told you, this is the new frontier of deer. It hasn't been civilized by years and decades and centuries of use. But the results have been good enough for me that I'm sure they'll help you, too. So why not spread the word so we all can have some fun with it?

Deer in Distress

Most mammals have soft hearts when it comes to the cry of a baby. After viewing creatures of the outdoor world, and with no sexist bias, I'll add that this is especially true of the females of the species. If you don't believe it, just pay attention to human behavior the next time you go to church, to the shopping mall or to a meeting. Once a baby starts crying, no one seems to be able to ignore it, especially the mothers in the crowd. As the crying continues, heads begin to turn. And if the baby proves to be alone without anyone

Does just can't seem to ignore the sound of a fawn in distress.
Frank R. Martin photo.

to help it, someone and possibly many someones will head over there to try to help it.

The same thing is true among deer. The sound of a crying fawn does not go unnoticed. It will draw some kind of reaction from every deer in the area. It will especially draw the attention of does.

They might rally to its defense. They might take it as a danger signal and run away. They might come close first and then run away. But it's guaranteed—deer will react strongly.

In terms of deer calling, we call that sound of a crying fawn a distress call. Delivered as high-pitched wails and with some urgency, it sounds as if a fawn is starving to death, being attacked by a pack of vicious predators or is in immediate peril from some other danger. Delivered that way, the distress call is a powerful stimulus. In fact, sometimes it can be too powerful.

Gordon Eastman gave the best description of the brightest side of a distress call at work when he told me about using the sound while filming deer in the early summer, the time when young fawns were about. There were no deer in sight when he set up his camera and started blowing the call. Almost immediately, a doe rushed in. She alternately stopped and then dashed back and forth in a field of tall grass looking for the fawn she was trying to defend. As the calling continued, other does came in and did the same. It made for some dramatic film footage for the video "How to Talk to the Deer."

On the other end of the spectrum, there was one of my first experiences with calling in fawns. It happened during the hunting season and the fawns in this story were alone at the time. Since it was early in the rut, I figured their mother had probably wandered off with a buck to do some courting. In any event, I sat down and began calling them up the hill toward me using soft common doe sounds. As they got closer, I could hear them calling back to me until eventually, the pair was just below me, less than ten feet away. From the time I first could hear their calls, I began imitating the sound they made. In turn, they ignored me, looking around instead for the doe they thought was calling to them. When they got in close, I decided to try a distress call. I can tell you that the last time I saw them, they were still running full-bore as they cleared the next ridgeline, heading out as fast as they could. It was a prime example of blowing the wrong call at the wrong time.

The distress sounds Gordon and I were making in each of these stories were exactly the same call. One time, the deer came in at a dead run. The other time, they ran away with equal speed. As I said, the call is powerful. And, I should add, not always predictable.

The distress sound is really nothing more than a rapid and louder version of the common doe sound. It's in the volume and speed with which it's delivered that it generates its power. In fact, in the scheme of deer calling, it's the only call you can make in which a loud delivery isn't really a concern.

How loud can you make a distress call and still have it work? You'll be shocked to find out.

One day, a friend of mine in Colorado was watching one of Gordon's videos on how to call in deer with a friend of his who is a rodeo announcer. The following morning, the rodeo announcer was testing out his sound system at the rodeo arena in Steamboat Springs. As part of the test, the announcer began blowing the call over the microphone and the arena's public address system. Before he was done with the test, he had called a group of mule deer into the rodeo arena, past the bucking chutes, right up to the speakers which were broadcasting his call.

That may sound strange. But the story really didn't surprise me. While I've never tried it myself with the deer call, I witnessed the same thing years ago when I amplified a tape of a bugling bull elk and boomed it out of one of those portable predator-calling loudspeakers over and over again. In Montana, it isn't legal to use an electronic device like that for hunting purposes and I wasn't hunting at the time. But it certainly was something to see when a bull elk came right over and was nose-to-speaker with the unit. The tape was bugling so often and the unit was so loud that the whole situation was anything but authentic in its presentation. Yet that bull elk didn't mind.

The deer in the rodeo arena were in a similar situation. It wasn't really very real. In fact, if I were in a hunting situation I'd never even consider that much volume. But sometimes, with a distress call, you can get away with it.

As I said, however, the danger in a distress call is that you're never sure how the deer are going to react. Sometimes, it will bring them in faster than using common doe sounds. Other times, it can have the reverse effect and you scare the animals away.

One way to get around that is to make three or four of the soft common doe sounds first, then go to your distress call. The common doe sounds will establish for any deer within calling range that there are some deer in the area. Then,

Adam McMullin made the most of a deer that stopped to hear the call.
Jerry Gillum photo.

when you go to the distress call, they won't be instantly alarmed by it.

Another thing you should understand about the distress call is that it generally works very poorly for calling in bucks. Does are the ones likely to be lured in by it and older does in particular are most likely to be attracted.

My own experiences with distress sounds tell me that the does most likely to respond are the older does in a group. Just as a cow call often calls in the lead cow in a group, the deer call brings in the lead doe. When she comes in, she may very likely bring in the rest of her little herd with her. If there's a buck in the group, he'll likely come, too. But as for lone bucks or bachelor bunches of bucks, they may pick up their heads and look in your direction, but they'll very rarely come in. Again based on my experiences with the call, I can't say that the bucks won't ever come. I'll just say that the distress call doesn't work as consistently on them as it works on does.

Just because it doesn't lure them in, however, doesn't mean that the distress call shouldn't be used by buck hunters. You'll need the distress sound. It just won't be needed in the same way.

What you need to develop in your calling is something of a half-distress call. It's not the soft and low sound of the common doe call. It's not the rapid, loud sounds of a distress call. It's something in between and, for lack of a better name, I've called it the half-distress call. It's just a little louder than the common doe sound and delivered with a little more urgency.

In earlier parts of this book, we talked about using a deer call to stop a deer that's running away from you. The half-distress call is the one you rely on for that task. Why it works, I don't know. What it's telling the fleeing deer, I don't know. But it's something they respond to.

When you have a buck running away from you, just start blowing the half-distress call. Almost invariably, a buck hearing that sound will stop, turn around and look at you. He may only stand there for a few seconds before he starts running again, but if you're hunting that deer and following him in your sights, those few seconds are long enough to deliver a good, standing shot.

The only danger in using that half-distress sound is that it might take some planning to deliver it effectively. One of the more frustrating things I've learned about it is that if there is any cover at all near the deer when he hears the call, he's going to stop behind that cover to take his look back. As a result, you have to plan ahead for about how long it's going to take for the call to reach the deer's ears—usually about two seconds—and not have the sound get there when he's close to cover. Often, you're better off to let the deer run past the cover before you blow the call and hope he doesn't find anything else to hide behind.

That kind of behavior, stopping and looking back at what could be a dangerous situation, was usually thought of as a trait only among mule deer. Because they do it so often, whether you call to them or not, the mule deer have been typified as being stupid.

With a half-distress call, I've done the same thing with whitetails, however, and taken nice bucks because of it. And no one has ever insulted the whitetails for lack of intelligence.

The truth of the matter is simply that deer are programmed to react to the sound of another deer in distress or, in the buck's case, something that can only be described as half-distress. They might react by coming near. They might react by running away. They might even react by stopping. All I can tell you for sure is that if you make these sounds, the deer will react in some way to your call and because of that, it's one of the most powerful sounds that a caller can make.

Common Doe Sounds

The basis for all deer calling should be the common doe sound. It's simple. It's a one-note monotone. It's short in duration. It's nothing more than a "naaah."

Yet if the distress call holds power for the deer caller, the common doe sound holds mystery for the deer. It's in that mystery that a deer caller can lure in deer of all ages, both sexes and in all seasons.

The common doe sound is my name for this call. You won't find it called that in the literature on deer and deer hunting. In the same way, you won't find the literature calling something a half-distress call. But I had to call them something and the terms common doe sound and half-distress call seemed to fit the bill.

The reason I call this one the common doe sound is that it seems to form the basis for all communication in deer. As I said before, it's the basic sound that fawns make when they're young. It's the same basic sound that does and bucks make when they're older. All deer seem to say it, whether it's high-pitched and short when the deer are fawns or deeper and longer when they get older.

When I started researching the sound for my Deer Talk call, the common doe sound was what I was really looking for—an all-purpose deer sound that the animals responded to. What I found out instead was that deer make many different sounds. And even what I eventually sorted out as the common doe sound wasn't always made the same way.

Sometimes, the common doe comes out clear. Other times, it's more of a nasal sound. After watching the animals, I found out why. Sometimes, the deer make the call with their mouths open. Other times, they do it with their mouths shut. With the mouth shut, it takes on more of a nasal tone. Either way, it seems to have the same effect when deer hear it.

Exactly what the common doe sound is saying to the deer is anyone's guess. All I know is that deer relate to it as a sound that deer make. Its effects on the deer vary as well. It tends to gather them. It tends to calm them down. It makes them look for other deer. But most of all, it interests them enough that they want to discover its source.

Don Snyder, a friend in Colorado, found out just how well it worked in attracting and holding deer last fall when he took his two sons out hunting during a special doe season on the eastern slopes of the Rockies. The hunt began with a long missed shot by the older boy when they misjudged a 300-yard herd of deer as a 400-yard herd of deer and took aim over the top of a mule deer doe's back. At the shot, the deer scattered and disappeared into a big basin.

Don, who had been playing around with one of my calls, began blowing it. He didn't see any deer when he started.

When deer hear a common doe sound, they often gather together.
Jim Hamilton photo.

But in a short time, the deer began appearing and before long, there were fifty deer within view. Don's younger boy, who had never shot a deer before, was next up for a shot. But frankly, the young boy was a bit too excited. As Don kept calling, the young boy shot...and shot...and shot until he emptied the gun. Don kept calling as the gun was reloaded and the deer stayed in the area. So the boy shot...and shot...and shot and emptied the gun again without touching a hair of a deer. Believe it or not, the boy reloaded and emptied the gun again before Don decided to let the older boy have another chance and a doe was downed.

The following day, Don and his boys returned to the drainage and called again. Once again, all the deer (minus one) showed up. This time, the younger boy made a clean shot and got his deer. But Don told me that even as the boy shot, he could see more deer filtering out of the cover in the basin to come to the call. He added that all the missing the day before was simply a matter of too much excitement and too many deer. His young son just went from deer to deer to deer, missing them all.

In my own experiences with the common doe sound, I've had much the same type of experience. It seems that even when you're out in the open and the deer can see you, they tend to look past you searching for the deer that they're sure is making the noise. Like all calling situations, however, the common doe sound does work better if the deer can't see you. But just because you have been spotted doesn't necessarily mean a deer won't come.

One of the key things to remember when using common doe sounds is to be patient. With elk calls, deer calls and turkey calls, everyone starts with the impression that the calls are going to work magic and bring in animals quickly. Actually, quite the opposite is true. The best callers, in fact, are usually the ones with the most patience who are willing to work the call and let the call work for them.

Another of the things you need to remember about making the common doe sound is that it simulates the natural conversation of other deer. For that reason, there really isn't a need for the deer to run in. They'll more often be wandering in slowly, searching with their eyes and noses and ears for the deer making the sound.

This tendency to wander in is especially true of bucks responding to the call. Often, I've watched them come in on a zig-zag course, trying to play the wind with their noses and working for positions where their eyes can see better. On one occasion in the mountains near home, I actually saw a young mule deer buck stand with his front legs up on a pine stump just so he could stand taller and get a better view in the direction the call was coming from.

If you're working on more than one deer, expect the deer

Deer will often wander and come in slowly to the common doe sound.
Frank R. Martin photo.

to move toward other animals in their herd when they first hear the call. To my way of thinking, they're checking each other out to see if the others are the source of the sound. Once the herd gathers, they might move in on you all in a group. But even if they don't, the call will have helped you.

Many times, I've seen a lone deer standing and blown the call only to find there were other deer nearby that I didn't see. When they heard the call, bedded deer stood up. Other deer that may have been hidden behind trees, brush or rocks stepped into view. Often, I've spotted bucks that were bedded nearby that I didn't even know were in the area.

While volume and urgency are the ingredients of the distress call, soft noises and less frequency are the keys to successful use of the common doe sound. Most novice callers blow the call too loud. They might also blow it too often.

What I like to do is start the calling softly, relying on the gathering power of a deer's big ears to hear my sounds. If I get no response, then I'll gradually build the volume in my calling until a deer hears me. Once he does hear me, I'll back off on the volume again.

It's the soft calls that seem to be the most mysterious to the deer. Perhaps it's because they can't hear the common doe sounds so well that they come in closer. Maybe they just want to hear it better.

I'll also try to disguise my calling position. Though deer have great hearing and the ability to pinpoint sounds with the radar-like scanning of their ears, it is possible to confuse them. One way I do it is to put my hand out in front of the call and deflect the sound so they don't hear it straight on. With the bounce off my hand, it can deflect the sound toward hills behind me or off of trees that may be nearby. In either case, the deer coming in will be looking for the location of the source of the call and his eyes will be focused on where he perceives that source to be. If there's a light breeze blowing, that further deceives the deer as to the source of the sound.

To get a more nasal-sounding call, I close the end of the call with my thumb and index finger. Rather than a clear common doe sound coming out, it takes on the same characteristics as a deer blowing the sound through his nose.

That's really about all there is to it. There are some other strategies you can use that will be discussed in the pages ahead. We'll pass on what we've learned about the call.

But the important thing is that all a caller really needs is three sounds — the distress call, half-distress call and the common doe sound. And of the three, the common doe sound is probably the most reliable when it comes to not alarming deer and bringing them close to you.

The other thing to remember is to be patient with your common doe sounds. They'll work only if you give them time to work. We'll get into calling schemes later and diagram some calling sequences, too. But you can have all the schemes and sequences you want and if you don't have the patience, they won't help you.

Just as you've heard the stories of elk and turkey hunters and predator callers who gave up their calling positions too

---

Doe Talk ■

quickly and spooked animals that were still coming in, the same thing is true of deer callers.

So keep your calling simple. Don't try to make every sound a deer makes. You don't need them. And have patience, for in the end, it's the patient hunter or wildlife photographer who is making good sounds that will be the most successful with a deer call.

Recipes for Success

Baking a chocolate cake has always been pretty easy for me. You just organize the flour, sugar, eggs, milk, baking powder and chocolate. Then you grab a cookbook and turn to the page on chocolate cakes. From there, you just follow the recipe. If you have all the right ingredients, in the right amounts, and you bake the cake the right length of time, you'll always turn out a great chocolate cake.

My experiences in the outdoors, however, have never been so cut-and-dried. Hard-and-fast rules tend to disintegrate in the realities of changing situations. Recipes tend to get muddled and changed. There are just too many variables like wind, weather and the animals involved that tend to make each situation just a little different.

So when it comes down to telling you exactly what you should be doing in deer hunting and deer calling, I'd be a fool to say that all you have to do is follow one set of rules and you'll always have the hunt of your dreams. Rather than giving you one recipe for success, my aim is to offer you tendencies in hunting and calling. I'll try to tell you what I did. I'll try to tell you what happened. I'll try to explain why those things happened. But from there, you'll have to do a little free-lance hunting and calling to fit your own situation.

In this section, you'll find some general calling strategies that have been successful. You'll find calling charts on time lines that will give you a starting point in your own efforts in the field. But from that point on, you'll be on your own to develop your own calling style, your own calling strategy and your own calling successes.

For some hunters, that concept of being on your own is a hard thing to swallow. Frankly, a lot of hunters lack the confidence in themselves. They're afraid to try something new, like a deer call, even if they've been told it works. The thing those people should remember is that all the successes or failures that they have in the field are for themselves only. There's no cheering section when you succeed. There's nobody to boo when you make a mistake. So if you do blow a situation, just look at it as a learning experience for next time. Laugh at the situation. Laugh at yourself. Then go on and try it all again. After all, the reason people are in the field hunting or photographing deer is for their own enjoyment. So grab your call, head into the field, and just have fun.

With that little lecture behind us, let's give you a starting point in your calling. If you want to call it something, call it your first recipe for success. I call it the deer information line — 555-1212.

Those numbers — 555-1212 — are the starting point I generally use when calling deer. They remind me about the type of calls to use and the timing required between those calls. It works like this: The three fives are three common doe sounds, spaced five seconds apart. The 1212 represents four half-distress sounds spaced one or two seconds apart. Then I wait 10 minutes and look for a response. When I repeat the sequence, I'll do it a little louder, thinking that perhaps the deer were outside of hearing range of my first series of calls. Again, I'll wait 10 minutes and look for a response.

The first time I used the sequence, I had the benefit of seven does within sight on a hillside about 200 yards away. None of them even lifted their heads at the first three common doe sounds. Their first reaction came with the 1212 at the end. Before I even finished the last half-distress call, some of the deer were already moving. Before I could get into the second sequence, all the deer were on the move toward me. Eventually, they came to a high fence that they didn't care to jump, but they were actually pushing against

The deer call has proven to work well for blacktail hunters.
Mike Schwiebert photo.

that fence with their bodies straining to see what was making the noise.

As I said, one of the real benefits of that situation was that
I had visual contact with the deer right from the start. I
could see them. They couldn't see me. Of all calling situations, that is the best. It's always much more difficult when
you're calling blind. That's true, in fact, whether you're
calling in deer, elk, turkeys or anything else.

Visual contact can be critical because more than anything
else, you're playing with a deer when you call to him or her.
And, rather than using a pat recipe, you're playing it by ear.
In its simplest terms, it works like this. Say, for example,

DEER CALLING — QUICK REFERENCE

STOPPING A RUNNING DEER

seconds	1	4	1	3	
sequence 1	C	D	D	D	sequence 2

If the deer does not stop on the first sequence of calling,
increase volume and use second sequence of calling.

*Note: By allowing two seconds for reaction time,
deer can be stopped in the open instead of behind secure cover.*

CALLING A DOE

seconds	1	7	13	15	17	18	20
	C	C	C	D	D	D	D

A doe will usually respond quickly to this type of calling. If they do not
respond, repeat sequence with more urgency on the distress sounds.

*Note: If the doe is coming in, stop your calling. Only call when the doe stops.
Calling in a lead doe will usually bring in the group she is with, bucks included.*

CALLING A BUCK

seconds	1	3	10
	C	C	C

Patience is the key to this type of calling.
Space this sequence of calling approximately five minutes apart.

*Note: Calling too loud can defeat your objective. If the buck is sighted,
call only when he hesitates and tone down your sounds as he approaches.
A buck will usually come in slow.*

MAKING DEER MOVE

seconds	1	5	10
	D	D	D

This sequence can be repeated as often as thought necessary.

*Note: Bedded deer will usually stand up.
Deer in cover will usually move to an open spot to look.*

Key: C-common doe sound   D-half-distress sound

*Note: Full distress sound are a quick series of half-distress sounds.
This sequence can be used for calling in does.*

Doe Talk ■

that the first sequence of calls you make catches the interest of the deer and it starts coming. If you blow the call again, the deer will stop to listen. Right there, you've defeated the purpose of your calling. The deer was coming. You stopped it by calling. Now, you've got to try to get the deer started again. The deer might start right up again. But it might not.

A far better scenario, and the one that has proven time and time again to be the most reliable for me, is to blow the call only after the deer stops. If the deer is coming, I keep quiet so it continues to close the distance between us. It's only when the deer stalls that I get back on the call.

Another rule of thumb is that as the deer gets closer, my calling gets softer and quieter. The rationale is the same as if you were coming in yourself to the cries of another person. If you're far away, that person might have to shout so you can hear him. As you get closer, you don't need the person to shout anymore.

In the case of a deer, with far superior hearing to our own, that animal doesn't need great volume anyway. The deer hears just fine. It hears things you can't. Besides, what you're trying to do is coax the deer closer. What you want is for the deer to have the impression that another deer is whispering to him. That way, the deer will come closer to find out what all the whispering is about.

To play a deer that way, the best situation is having visual contact with the deer you're calling to. If you're calling blind, you just have to hope you're making the right sounds at the right times. About the only safeguard you have against stopping deer that are moving in unseen is to space your calling sequences far apart. My suggestion is 10 minutes. That will give the deer plenty of time to react in between sequences. It will give you plenty of time to use your binoculars or strain your eyes to look for deer that might be responding.

Another tendency I have in my calling is to rely more heavily on the common doe sound when I don't have visual contact with deer. As I said before, this sound is more subtle than the distress or half-distress call. So if a deer is

Visual contact can be critical to knowing when to call to a deer.
Don Laubach photo

moving in, I'm much less likely to spook him out of the country than I would be with the louder, harsher calls.

I've also found this more infrequent pattern of calling to be better because I feel it's impossible to imitate the exact calling patterns of the deer themselves. Sometimes, the deer will go through long periods of time without ever uttering a sound. Other times, it's almost a constant chatter.

Doe Talk ■

One recent day in Gardiner, my wife and I were sitting on the porch of our home at the edge of town watching a group of mule deer feed nearby. The deer were well accustomed to us. They'd been feeding near our house all winter long. Most of the deer were just twenty or thirty yards away. But one that was about forty yards away suddenly started calling. It made the common doe sound about thirty or forty times with three-second intervals between each call. Not one of the feeding deer paid any attention to it. Finally the deer stopped calling and went to feeding itself.

It's anyone's guess as to exactly what that deer was saying or why it felt it needed to say it so often and in such rapid succession. Whatever it said, it didn't seem to have any effect on the feeding deer around it. And all it told me was that if I was going to call that frequently and make the common doe sound so often, that the deer were probably going to ignore me, too. Since then, I've just stayed away from rapid calling.

Adding more fuel to the theory that soft calls and infrequent calling are best is the fact that deer, like elk and turkeys, don't need to hear a sound more than once or twice before they have the source of that calling pinpointed. I've had elk come in from a half mile or more away, in the mountains, through dense timber, at the sound of a single series of calls. There's no reason to expect deer to be any different.

The thing to do is to give it a try. Don't be afraid to make a few mistakes. You'll learn from them. And don't just use the call during hunting season, either. You can often learn your calling lessons better out of season, when the pressure is off and when you have more time to learn than in the short weeks of the deer season. Just grab your camera, instead of your gun, and head for the hills.

One new friend from Billings did just that last season. I met the man just after giving a seminar on deer calling and he introduced himself by saying that he wanted to tell me something about my deer call. In situations like that, I'm always a bit hesitant. As often as not, someone has been blowing the call wrong and he's going to tell me about how it didn't work for him and how he wants me to tell him, in two minutes or less, how to do it right.

The man told me instead that his job was as a delivery driver and his route took him through some good deer country on his way to and from delivering packages. Over the course of the summer, he said he'd had a ball blowing the call. He'd talked to countless deer. Some of them he called right up to his truck. Others circled around the truck on the rural roads that made up his route.

During the first week of the hunting season, the driver had a chance to take his young son out for deer. Again, he used the call and brought in a five-point, western-count muley. But his son, being a young hunter, missed the big buck. The next time out, the driver used the call again and lured in a four-point this time. And this time, the boy connected.

Was the delivery driver happy about the call? He told me, "You'll never take my deer call away from me. You might get my wife. But you'll never get my deer call."

It went unsaid that perhaps the biggest reason for the man's success during the hunting season was his use of the call before the season ever began. He had learned his lessons well during the summer and when hunting season began, he knew what sounds to make and when to make them.

To me, it was exciting to find a fellow caller who shared the magic and became a true believer. Rather than following someone else's precise prescription for calling in deer, he had started with the basics, learned the way of the deer and the call in the field himself and come up with his own recipe for success. And I can tell you here and now, the same thing can happen to you.

BUCK TALK

Young Bucks, Old Bucks, No Bucks

I always have to laugh when people start talking about the good old days. Good old days? That's a matter of opinion. It's also a matter of timing. Believe me, the good old days weren't always so good.

I've talked with good-old-days hunters from the whitetail woods of Wisconsin to the mountain muley haunts of Montana and beyond. And when you talk to these good old boys at some depth, you'll quickly find that in many ways, we're much better off today in terms of deer than we ever were in the past.

Chalk it up to the benefits of good game management, the end of our homesteading days or hunters who are more respectful of the resource. But whatever the cause, deer are more plentiful today across most of their range than they ever were in the past.

A Wisconsin hunter now in his early seventies told me that he could remember the days when there were no whitetails in the southern half of that currently deer-rich state. If you worked in the industrial centers of the southern part of the state or farmed there and wanted to hunt deer, you had to drive at least a couple of hundred miles north and stalk them in the alder swamps and maple woods.

He could still remember, in fact, the first time he cut a deer track while hunting for ruffed grouse in the south. He was baffled by it, he told me. He wondered who had lost a sheep and why it was wandering in an alder swamp. It wasn't that the hunter didn't know what deer tracks looked like. It was the fact that there hadn't been any deer within a hundred miles of the spot since the early farmers, loggers and settlers had shot them all off.

Today in Wisconsin, you can find white-tailed deer everywhere from the sandy shores and big woods that border Lake Superior in the north to the golf courses, parks and suburbs of southern cities like Milwaukee, Racine, Kenosha and Madison. The hunting harvest annually goes over a quarter of a million deer. Hunters have the opportunity to take more than one deer. There are incentives for taking antlerless deer. And whitetails have become something of a pest in residential areas where animal rights activists, hunters, homeowners and game managers do battle over how, when, where and if they should control the deer situation.

The Wisconsin situation isn't an isolated one, either. Other eastern states have also found deer numbers on the rise where habitat is available for them. Just give whitetails a little security cover and some food and water and they'll carve out a niche they can live in. It doesn't matter if man happens to be living next door.

In the West, mule deer and whitetail numbers are also booming in ways that older hunters can hardly believe. In the old days, it just wasn't that way.

On the prairies of Montana, it was the coming of the railroad and the homesteaders of the early 1900s, combined with the drought of the Dirty '30s, that knocked down mule deer numbers. With several families of homesteaders to each section of land, there were few places where mule deer could hide. They were hunted for meat right on the farms. They were displaced by plowed fields. And they were pursued into the mountains in every season of the year. Mule deer and antelope all but vanished in the rush to settle the West.

What the hunters didn't get, the drought did. Periodic droughts are part of the history of the West and still affect deer numbers today. In years of little rain or snow, food supplies grow short. When tough winters follow these years of poor plant growth, animal mortality on the prairie can still reach 90 percent.

Old hunters will tell you that deer were so few in number on the prairies and even in the mountains that if you were lucky enough to cut a deer track, you followed it. You stayed on that track until you found the deer and shot it or until you lost the track. The reason you followed it with such intensity was because it was almost a sure thing that this would be the only set of tracks you'd find that day, or in some places, that season.

Pressure on those deer came from all sides. My grandparents, for example, homesteaded on Duck Creek at the base of the Crazy Mountains. Their log cabin was at one end of a ten-acre meadow that ran along the creek. At the other end of the meadow stood eight teepees where Indians lived. I can tell you that deer hunters came out of both ends of that meadow and ranged through the mountains and the prairies near them.

As a result of that pressure and the hunting from others nearby, deer were few in number and everyone who hunted them became an expert tracker. If their tracking skills weren't at the expert level, those hunters didn't come home with any deer.

In Montana, it wasn't until the 1940s that deer began to return in decent numbers. It wasn't until the 1960s that deer became truly numerous. And while deer numbers have fluctuated to some extent with the cycles of drought and tough winters since then, the situation today still has to be considered as among the best of this century.

While mule deer numbers have bounced back across the prairies and mountains of the West, whitetails have also

White-tailed deer weren't always as abundant as they are today.
Frank R. Martin photo.

made significant inroads. They thrive in agricultural areas, especially those where they can find some river-bottom brush and trees for cover to help them along. They've moved into some mountain areas, too, where they have often displaced the mule deer populations.

This invasion of whitetails has been another significant trend of the second half of the twentieth century in many parts of the West. Just how extensive the whitetail distribution will be during the twenty-first century is a matter of speculation that we'll leave to the experts and the passage of time. Suffice it to say that old-time hunters of the West are only beginning to adapt their hunting methods to take advantage of the situation. And hunters transplanted to the West from the East are finding some of the best whitetail hunting they've ever experienced.

While deer numbers and distribution have changed, so have the attitudes and tendencies of the hunters. For one thing, hunters are far more keyed into trophy deer today than they ever were before, especially in the West.

Huge antlers were more of a drawback than a plus in years past, when hunters were more concerned with putting meat on the table than putting antlers on the wall. Big antlers, in fact, meant that what you were shooting was an old deer. Old deer meant tough meat. So if you had the choice, you'd take a tender yearling or two-year-old. Those bucks provided the best eating.

Even the big buck contests have changed. Today, you're likely to have contests determined by the number of points that a buck has or by the Boone and Crockett scoring points that a buck can muster. In the old days, those contests were more often determined by weight. Hunters then were far more interested in how much meat a buck would put away for the winter than in how many hats his rack would hold.

I can remember in my boyhood that my dad and uncle were involved in just such a contest. They went into the Crazy Mountains near where my family lived. And my uncle shot what would today be considered nothing more than a three-point, western count, mule deer. The antlers on the buck were fairly heavy, but the deer was no trophy by today's standards. The thing about that deer, however, was that the three-point's body size was huge. My uncle ended up winning the big buck contest with it and putting 320 pounds of meat into the freezer.

In the years since then, I've looked high and low for a picture of that deer. I can remember the picture. My dad had shot a three-point that year, too, and the two deer were hanging from the hocks on their rear legs side by side on a meat pole. My dad's deer was an average three-point mule deer buck and its antlers just touched the ground. My uncle's deer, however, was so big that its shoulders, neck and head were all on the ground. It was a classic mountain mule deer, but it wouldn't even come close to winning a big buck contest today.

About all you can really say about the old days is that they were different. Hunting pressure might have been lighter in some parts of the country. It was certainly heavier in others. But overall, in most places, the good old days weren't really so good for deer after all.

Hunters of today have far more latitude in their opportunities than hunters of long ago. They can hunt big bucks for the wall if they so choose. They can still go after younger bucks for the table. And in some places, they even have multiple deer tag opportunities where they can hunt does for the table and bucks for the wall, all in the same season.

The thing to do is to make the most of your opportunities and enjoy the hunting we have available. Good game management and expanding deer herds have made mule and white-tailed deer more numerous in our lifetime than in the days of our grandparents and parents. In many ways, you'd have to say that we're living the good old days of deer hunting in the deer hunting of today.

Before the Rut

The wide-open highways of the West seem to be tailor-made for daydreaming. The highway patrol might not appreciate that remark. But it's true. And, I'll admit, I just can't help it.

When I feel that first twinge of morning frost in the weeks of early fall, my head starts spinning toward hunting season. As I look at the miles of open road ahead of me, my heart leaps and my imagination soars.

Inevitably, my thoughts return to a crisp September evening in a mountain range not far from Helena, Montana. I was bowhunting. The day was coming to an end. But before I began my final descent from a high ridge toward the trail that would lead me to my waiting car, I stopped for a while and watched the night descend on the valley below.

As the light began to fail, I saw headlights being switched on as vehicles rolled down distant highways. I saw ranch lights come on and glow in the gathering gloom. And I saw the city far away come to life with lights. With the first cool

Hunters have a choice over what type of buck they care to shoot.
Jerry Gillum photo.

puffs of evening wind blowing down the ridge behind me, I felt the damp night air begin dropping into the valley below. I watched the first stars appear, twinkling faintly at first, then growing in intensity as others joined them in the clear sky above.

The scene was breathtaking. I just had to take it in for a time before I roused my tired legs and headed down the slope toward home. But even as I made my final descent of the day, my mind wandered back to the high country behind me where I'd spent the past dozen hours in search of deer and elk. Somewhere back there, with barely enough light still showing to illuminate him, a big mule deer buck was just now rousing himself from his bed. With legs still

Buck Talk ■

stiff from a day spent at rest, he'd rise to his feet. He'd stretch those legs and shake his heavy-antlered head. And finally, he would step out into view to begin the nocturnal life that the truly big bucks often lead.

Now that the hunters were gone, and I was gone with them, he would begin his day even as the humans of the world were ending theirs. By morning, when my feet would be carrying me back to the high country, his day would be ending in the same bed or one nearby. And he'd be safe once more.

It's always a beautiful vision to share with a wide-open highway in the weeks before hunting season. And, no doubt, it's a true vision, too.

The simple fact about hunting bucks before the rut is that you're going to be hunting them while they're at their best. You're going to be hunting them on their own turf. And you're going to be hunting them when the odds are all stacked in their favor.

I've always maintained that the most difficult trophy of them all to take is a big mule deer buck early in the season. And if you're hunting them really early with a bow and arrow, you've got a gargantuan task ahead of you.

During the weeks of September and October, you don't have the breeding season to make them silly. You don't have the snows to drive them to lower ground. You don't have the food shortages that can be caused by deep snow or winter range conditions.

The truth of the matter, too, is that you literally have to go after the big bucks, if you can find them in the first place. That, in itself, can be a trick.

In the mountains, mule deer bucks often head to the highest and most remote country they can find. The key for them is to find an area that meets all their security and food needs within a relatively small area. That way, they don't need to wander very far to find the necessities of life and expose themselves to hunters along the way.

How remote and site-specific can these places be? A bowhunting friend of mine, Rob Seelye, once told me about

before the rut, you're hunting bucks in their own home territory. Frank R. Martin photo.

just such a place he found that owed its existence to a giant snowdrift.

That snowdrift clung to a high north slope at the very top of a mountain range in Montana. It would build in size all winter long, getting deeper and deeper with the dumping of fresh snow and the blowing of the wind. Then, as spring arrived, all the snow around it would melt and it, too, would begin to melt slowly in the shade of the steep, high slope.

In most years, by the following September there would be just enough of that snowdrift left to produce trickles of water cascading in tiny fingers down the slope. That water would keep the grasses green at that spot, even when all the surrounding hills turned brown and dry. That water also provided a cooling drink for the mule deer all through the hot summer and into the fall. And the steep nature of the slope itself, along with its remote location, provided a secure home for the deer. As a result, the place grew some monstrous mule deer for anyone who happened to find this

Buck Talk ■

little hidey-hole.

The first year Rob found the spot, he and a couple of his friends took some huge bucks out of the spot with their rifles. But because the place wasn't very big and the big bucks could have been shot out in just a few seasons, the hunters made a pact with each other. They'd hunt that place only with their archery gear. With that restriction on themselves, they never have repeated the success of the first year there with so many deer. But they've got a spot they can return to anytime they want where they know the big bucks will be. And with bows and arrows in hand, they can challenge themselves to take an early season mule deer buck, at close range, on his own turf.

At the time Seelye was developing his hunting strategies in this high mountain hidey-hole, he had to build his tactics around the trails the big bucks used heading to and from that snowdrift and the green grasses it fed. No effective deer call was available at the time.

If he heads there now, it would be interesting to see if his luck would improve with the ability to bring deer within range with the call. From my own experiences, I can tell you that using common doe sounds can help a great deal during the weeks before the rut, both in calling them in and in holding them while you move toward them.

Last fall for example, another friend, Murphy Love, was working the call on mule deer in Wyoming when we spotted three bucks in the velvet, all of them big bucks and one of them with a legitimate thirty-inch spread between his heavy antlers. Gordon Eastman and Murphy worked on those deer, using the call mostly as a cover to help mask their movements.

It worked this way. The three bucks were on the far side of a deep ravine. Gordon and Murphy were on the close side with little cover to hide them. So they stayed low, crawling on their hands and knees and blowing the call as they moved closer and closer. Eventually, they made it to the edge of the ravine and the three bucks were right across from them.

Because of the depth of the ravine, which would have taken the deer out of sight when they dropped to the bottom, the three bucks wouldn't come across. But for the next half hour, they played a game of hide and seek, wandering away for a time only to return to the edge and look back across at Gordon and Murphy. A good bowman could have had any of them. They were only forty to fifty yards away. But with the ravine between Gordon and Murphy and the deer, they wouldn't cross and come any closer.

As I said, the biggest of the bucks was a thirty-incher. I can tell you that because he eventually did fall last season and the deer call proved to be his undoing. He was 200 yards out during the rifle season and Murphy was working the area as an outfitter and called him to within 100 yards, where his client shot the big buck. Would the big buck have come closer? It's a moot point. The big buck was still coming when the hunter shot. But 100 yards with today's big game rifles is definitely close enough to make a good shot and put a buck down.

Mule deer bucks aren't the only ones that can't seem to tear themselves away from the common doe sound, either. Another Wyoming outfitter was using the call before the rut to lure whitetails out of the brush so his clients could see them.

In this case, the outfitter knew the brushy river bottom where the whitetails would hide. All he did was to set up where he could get a clear view of the edge of that brush. Then he'd begin making common doe sounds and use his binoculars to scan the brush before him.

He told me the call would attract both bucks and does that would come out to see what was making the sounds. Some of the hunters he guided would see the whitetails they wanted and shoot them right there. Others would see the whitetails they wanted and miss. At times, he even called the missed deer back again for a second miss, or even a third.

It was interesting to note that the outfitter said these whitetails, in the weeks before the rut, would rarely come in fast. They'd come in slow and sneaky. It might take

Big bucks often die of old age if they're not taken during the rut.
Frank R. Martin photo.

twenty minutes to bring them out of hiding. It might take thirty or forty or even fifty minutes. But as long as he knew the area he was calling to was holding deer, he'd stick with his calling and the whitetails would eventually come.

The key to success with the whitetails and mule deer both was knowing where they'd be hiding in the first place.

You've got to find the deer areas first, before you find the deer. All the calling in the world isn't going to help if there aren't any deer within earshot.

That means you have to know the habits and lifestyles of the deer you plan to hunt. You have to know where whitetails will be and why they'll be there. You have to be able to identify a mule deer hideout when you stumble onto it.

In short, the deer call is a great tool for luring in deer or holding them so you can get closer. But you can't expect instant success with it if you don't have some solid hunting skills to go along with it. Being a good hunter entails knowing and being skilled with all pieces of the puzzle, not just the one involving a deer call. Just as I said, in the weeks and months before the rut, you have to hunt them on their own turf and when they're at their best. And even with a call to help you along, you've got your work cut out for you.

The Rut Is On

Of all times during the year, you stand the best chance of seeing the biggest bucks during the rut. The timing of this breeding season for whitetails and mule deer will vary, depending on what part of the country you happen to be hunting. It might start in mid-October. It might not peter out until mid-December. It might be at its peak anytime in between. But whenever the rut is on, your odds of seeing the biggest bucks improve immeasurably.

It's during this time that the bucks will be courting does pretty much around the clock. In a whitetail woods that I hunt, if I hit it right at the peak of the rut, this means that I can literally expect a buck to come through my stand at any hour of the day. I've seen almost as many chasing does on the brushy ridgetops at noon as I have at dawn and dusk. From the tracks left in the snow, I can tell they've been chasing them all night, too. Mule deer will be doing much the same. Instead of one buck chasing one doe like I find in the whitetail woods, however, it will be one or more bucks and a herd of does. The buck will be just as persistent, how-

Mule deer bucks will pursue a doe to determine if she's ready to breed.
Bob Zellar photo.

ever, moving from doe to doe to check them for readiness to breed. When he finds one that's close, he'll often stay with her, walking behind in the same way that a puppy follows its master.

In addition to being more visible during this time of year, bucks also are less wary. Sometimes, it seems, they'll do the stupidest things. Rather than be afraid or even aware of the hunter, they'll stick with the does. Often, that means the end for them.

I can remember, for example, taking my middle son, Kirk, out on a hunt for his first deer during the rut a number of years ago. We spotted a group of deer in a mountain drainage and began to work our way over to them to get a better look. But we were still 200 yards away when the deer spotted us and began to get edgy.

There was a buck in the group—a good three-by-four muley—but I'll admit that the odds of Kirk hitting him at that distance were not great. Excited by the situation and new at the hunting game, Kirk lined up his shot as well as he could. But he missed the buck entirely.

At the shot, and urged on by the three other shots Kirk took while emptying his gun, the herd of deer took off and went across the draw into another drainage. I figured we lost our chance at those deer for good. But the rut comes late in the hunting season here, so we decided to try to follow them up anyway.

In most situations like that, an older buck will put plenty of distance between himself and a hunter. But in this case, that buck was far more interested in keeping the company of those does than he was in staying away from us. As a result, when the does settled down not far past the ridgetop, the buck settled down too. Kirk got a second chance at the buck, and this time his nerves had calmed and he didn't miss.

If it hadn't been for the rut, there's no doubt in my mind that we'd never have had that second chance. But a buck in the rut doesn't operate like bucks in the pre-rut period. They make those kinds of mistakes. And the hunter who remains ready when the mistakes are made will often be rewarded for his vigilance.

Deer callers also stand to benefit from the fact that the bucks are totally smitten with does at this time of year. One benefit comes into play because the bucks are so intent on finding willing does. The other benefit is that the bucks are so willing to follow the does wherever they go.

I saw both benefits work in a single calling setup on a single field in Wyoming two years ago with Gordon Eastman. And we weren't even hunting that day. We were just shooting some film of the Deer Talk call in action.

After spotting some mule deer in the distance in an open field, I crawled down a shallow draw to work closer to them. There, laying down in the tall grass just below the lip of a little hump, I started to call. The first deer to respond to the sound was a big four-point. Leaving the other deer behind, he came straight downwind and across that big open field in search of the source of the common doe

Buck Talk ■

sounds. I watched him come to the edge of the draw, then drop out of sight as he stepped into it.

Since I couldn't see him anyway, I just kept my head down and called. Finally, I peeked out from under the brim of my hat. I was shocked. All I could see was the deer from the knees on down, not more than ten or fifteen feet away from me. That big four-by-four mule deer was right there within spitting distance. I didn't dare look up at him.

Eventually, the big buck must have felt that something was wrong because he began to walk away. At fifty yards, I blew on the call again and the sound started him to circling me, hoping to get to the downwind side. Finally, I scared him off on purpose. I just put up my hand and waved it at him. That buck ran 400 yards as fast as he could go. But I stayed there and called some more and, in twenty minutes, I had called him back in again, though not as close as the first time.

My own theory on it is that the buck was looking for a receptive doe and I must have sounded like one. He came in alone looking for love.

But as I said, my calling worked two ways that day. After playing with the big four-point, I was in for an even bigger surprise when my calling caught the attention of a doe out in that field. She came in too, to a distance of about forty or fifty yards. That she came in didn't surprise me. But she had a buck that trailed along after her that was nothing short of amazing.

In looking at Gordon's film later, we determined that the buck was actually a six-by-six and the spread on his wide, heavy rack must have been at least thirty inches. He was a certifiable monster that would have easily ranked well into the Boone and Crockett Club record book.

In this case, it was the doe that I had actually called in. But because it was the rut, the buck had trailed along after her. He had put himself in a vulnerable position simply because of the company he was keeping.

Could I have called him in by himself? Possibly. After all, I had called in the big four-point. But in the weeks before

Big bucks will come out of their hiding places to court does.
Jim Hamilton photo.

the rut, when he would have been much wiser, it would definitely have been a different situation. He might have come in. He might not have. But I sure had him in close now.

In some states, you don't have a choice as to whether or not you can hunt the rut. If the season is a short one, you simply hunt the open season. In other states, like Montana, the season is a long one that spans both the pre-rut period and the rut itself.

If you have a choice, the rut is definitely the time to be out in search of a big buck. There are many hunters here who purposely keep their deer guns tucked safely away in their gun cabinets until the rut arrives. They'll hunt birds, ducks, other big game animals or even go fishing just so they won't be tempted to shoot at a deer.

One such hunter I knew was a big buck gambler who annually saved his week of vacation for the last week of the Montana season. That week, which annually straddles the

Buck Talk ■

Thanksgiving holiday, would insure that he was hunting the big buck period. And the man found big bucks.

One year, when I hunted with him, he talked long and hard to get me to pass up a shot at a buck he didn't think was big enough. The buck was in the company of about fifteen does and was working his herd in a bowl nestled on the edge of a high ridge. Finally, I told my hunting partner that this buck was definitely big enough for me.

My stalk was a precarious one. The deer were high above me. All I had was a twisting little ravine which would hide me well in some places and leave me almost naked to the deer in others. To make matters worse, one of the does in the group spotted me when I was still 400 yards from the herd. All I could do was continue to move slowly and carefully and low, moving from one piece of cover to the next.

For some reason, that doe never spooked. She just kept watching me whenever the cover let her as I cut the distance between myself and the deer in half. At 200 yards, I finally had a good rest and a clear shot. I dumped the buck with a single shot.

This buck that was too small for my friend turned out to have a five-by-seven-point rack with an inside spread just shy of twenty-eight inches. It was no record-book head. Its rack lacked the true heaviness that Boone and Crockett bucks have. But the tines were long and beautiful. The outside dimensions of the rack were spectacular. And the body size of the deer left it in the 200-pound-plus class which made it more than a small challenge when it came to dragging it the mile or more back to the truck.

How could my friend be so picky? To his way of thinking, the buck wasn't a big one. His personal best at that time was a buck with a spread just shy of thirty-eight inches. He was searching for one that went forty inches and, a time or two, he thought he actually saw one that big, though he has yet to hang his tag on one.

What my friend realized, however, was the potential for shooting a big buck during the rut. It's the one time of the year when the big bucks come out of hiding and show themselves with some degree of regularity. It's a time when you stand a chance of calling in a big buck or a doe with a big buck trailing behind her. It's a time when even the biggest bucks will make mistakes that a hunter can capitalize on. In short, it's a time when big dreamers have an excellent chance of making their big dreams come true.

Trophy Bucks

For most hunters, the dreams start coming in the last few weeks before the deer season opens. In the middle of the night, in the middle of their sleep, these visions start drifting through their dreams. Perhaps it's a heavy-horned whitetail, all gray around the muzzle and wide through the hindquarters. Or maybe it's a mule deer with a rack so wide and tall that you can't lay a rifle in it and have it touch both main beams.

Trophies are like dreams. You can't really direct them. You can't know when they're going to drift into your life or what happens to them when they drift away. All you can do is hope that the dreams come in the night to sweeten your sleep. Then, you can hope those dreams come true when you have a gun or bow in your hand and a license in your pocket.

Trophy bucks hold that kind of mystery for hunters. Whether the individual hunter favors mule deer or whitetails, they are the elusive phantoms that many will dream about and few will ever realize.

There are reasons why trophy bucks are so hard to come by. For one thing, they are, indeed, rare. I had a talk with a wildlife biologist once whose business was to classify the mule deer of an entire mountain range which stretched for perhaps thirty miles in length and ten miles in width. He had studied the deer in that mountain range for several years. And he knew the places the deer would be in every season. There were plenty of deer in those mountains, he assured me. Yet when I talked to him about how many true trophy bucks the mountain range held, his eyes dropped

Trophy bucks are rare because of the things it takes to make them.
Jim Hamilton photo.

and his mouth curled into a smile. "Boone and Crockett-type trophies? Ones that will make the record book?" he asked.

That was what I was after. "There are a lot of nice four- and five-points in those mountains. But record-book bucks? There might be two," he replied.

I know from talking to the biologist that the mountain range must have held several thousand deer. Its far reaches were rugged, remote and truly wild in every sense of the word. Yet even in this wild and rugged place with so many deer, only two mule deer bucks could crack the record book. And, he might have added, they'd crack the book only if a hunter was lucky enough to find them and make a good shot.

The rarity of trophy bucks is caused by the things it takes for them to grow so big. They need the genes of big bucks in their history. They need good nutrition. They need good physical condition. And, perhaps most of all, they need the years behind them to grow big.

Some areas have better genetics than others. Big bucks have come from there before. To find them, just go to the record books that you hope to make, whether that's nation-wide in the annals of the Boone and Crockett Club or Pope and Young Club or in the records of the game department of your own individual state. That's easy enough.

As to nutrition and physical condition, that's not as easy to control. Antlers, for example, are just one part of a buck and not really the most important part, either. A buck that's starving is going to find the things he eats being used by his body to protect itself first and put into antler growth second.

It only stands to reason then that you can't expect superior antler growth in summers after extremely tough winters. The deer's vitality will have been pulled down so far by the winter that even on good summer range, it will take them time to recover. During that recovery period, the antler growth will suffer.

You won't get the most out of antlers during times of drought in the West or in years of particular food shortages, like acorn crop failures, for example, in the East. Bucks on short rations won't grow antlers as big as those that have all the food they could want.

The physical condition of the deer extends beyond the food needs, too. If a buck has damaged his testicles, he might grow freak horns and never shed the velvet. Some of these turn into so-called cactus bucks, which grow a cluster of short spikes that are never shed and never lose their vel-vet. Other times, the beams and points may grow intact, but still remain covered with velvet all through the hunting sea-son. If a buck bumps the antlers hard during their growth period, that too can result in deformities or freak growth. And there are some bucks whose pedicels, the places where

Bucks have to elude hunters for many seasons to grow to trophy size.
Frank R. Martin photo.

the antlers sprout, have been damaged and won't grow a decent rack.

While all of these factors limit the number of bucks that will enter the ranks of trophies, time is perhaps the biggest factor at work today. It takes a buck, even with all the growth factors above in place, about five to seven years to become a trophy. A four-year-old might be big enough to make it. An eight- or nine-year-old might still have enough vitality to keep his antlers in shape. But for the most part, it's the bucks between five and eight years old that are at the peak of their prime.

With so many hunters in so many places, that's a long time for a buck to survive. He'll have had to survive the high mortality year of his birth. He'll have had to make it past the firing line that takes so many bucks when they're one and two years old. And, when he starts his career as a prime breeding buck at ages three and four, he'll have to cope with the hard times of winter after running off all his fat reserves chasing does during the rut. With no fat reserves left, he'll have to hang on as well as he can each winter, hoping that he makes it through the lean times until he can fatten up again in spring.

At every turn, the deck is stacked against a buck reaching an age when he could be a trophy. A buck has to get smart quickly and learn the tactics it takes to survive. For the hunter seeking that buck, he, too, has to learn hunting strategy and become smarter to take a trophy.

Survival for a whitetail buck often means outwitting man in his own backyard. It's strategy relying on sneakiness, rather than the remoteness of his existence, that will help this species of buck to survive.

A friend of mine who hunts river bottoms of the West said he has seen big whitetails show some amazing talents to survive hunting seasons. The bottoms he hunts are invariably agricultural areas with patches of cottonwood timber, willows and nasty thickets of thornbushes and rosebushes. While organized drives through those areas will often run the does, fawns and smaller bucks toward waiting hunters, they rarely work on the big bucks.

Buck Talk ∎

He has seen those bucks wiggle themselves under tight mats of thorns and stay there, even when the drivers passed within a few feet of them. He has watched them crawl on their bellies just so they'd stay low enough to keep out of sight in a shallow ditch. And he has witnessed their weaving through patches of cover just to backtrack through a line of drivers, rather than running out front and facing the waiting guns.

The only time you'd ever catch one of those trophies out in the open was in the dimmest light of morning and evening — if you could catch them out then. More often, they'd hang back in the brush and wait until full dark to move out into the fields with the other deer for their nightly feeding.

It has been said, and rightly so, that most of these trophy whitetails die of winter kill and old age, rather than at the hands of a hunter. I believe it. I believe, too, that many of these whitetails are never even spotted by a hunter during the season.

While whitetails rely on stealth, mule deer are more apt to be preserved by the remoteness of the country in which they live. Big mule deer bucks of the mountains are most often found high above timber line, living in the same rugged places where you'd expect to find only bighorn sheep and mountain goats.

One time, in fact, I was up goat hunting in September and had climbed clear to the top of a mountain only to find a group of big mule deer bucks up there. They were bedded on a ridge where the early fall breezes would keep the flies away from them. It was the perfect spot where no one would normally look for them.

Another time, I went with two friends on horseback and rode eight miles back in from the end of the road to the head of a big basin. We had gone there to set up camp and look for elk. Instead, what we spotted were big mule deer bucks clear up in the shale rock slopes. There were enough small patches of scrub timber and grassy pockets to feed and hide them.

Even after spotting the bucks with our binoculars and spotting scopes, it still took us a full day to get up to where they were. In the end, one of our party even bagged a nice buck out of there. But the bucks had put themselves into a spot where getting one was far from an easy hunt.

Still another time, late in the fall, I was tracking some elk in the high country that took me clear to the head of a big canyon. The going was tough. In some places, the snows of fall had piled up clear to my waist. By the time I got to the head of the canyon, there was just enough daylight to turn around and head back.

But before I left, I decided to take out my binoculars and look around. What I saw in that world of deep snow were three huge mule deer bucks, using the windblown and sun-melted south-facing slopes to hang on before hard winter and the urges of the rut would force them down the mountain.

Remote country? You bet. That's one of the reasons they were able to live long enough to get big. Their isolation from other deer and the fact they were living so high also reduced the chances they'd be preyed upon by mountain lions, who most likely would have ranged down lower where there were more deer for them to take.

Just as the big whitetail bucks learned that stealth and patience would help them survive, the big mule deer bucks also learned that staying put in the face of danger was a reliable defense.

The best example of how tight a big buck can sit in hopes that danger won't spot him was shown to me on a bighorn sheep hunt some years back. At the time, I was using my spotting scope extensively to locate sheep, which can be tough to spot when they're bedded against the backdrop of gray mountain rock.

Eventually, I spotted a small cave with an animal bedded down inside it. Because of the distance and the shadows, I couldn't get a good look at the animal. But I felt sure it was probably a sheep which had found shelter and protection by bedding down inside.

Buck Talk

It took me an hour and a half to work into position for a closer look at the animal, taking me far down the mountain and then back up again. I had hoped to come down on him from above, but that way I wouldn't have been able to see him until I was right at the cave. So I came up from below until I was in a position some eighty yards away from the cave.

Looking at the animal again, I realized it was a big mule deer buck. With the time it took to hunt and then get into position to see inside the cave, there wasn't much daylight left. I had just about enough time to get back to camp. But I figured that at least I'd teach that mule deer buck a lesson before I left. I took aim with my rifle at the rocks above the cave and touched off a shot to spook him. While the bullet smashed home and sprayed rocks, the big buck never moved. So I shot again, rocking the mountainside with the blast and creating another spray of rocks. Once again, the mule deer buck didn't budge. So I shot one more time with the same results. Finally, I stood up and started climbing toward the cave. Only then did the big buck bolt from his bed and run off.

It was amazing. Three rifle shots from close range and, even then, the big buck didn't move. It took the positive sighting of a man coming toward him at close range before the big buck abandoned his position. It made me wonder how many other hunters could have worked over that mountainside and never spotted the buck. It made me wonder if other deer had been shot and fallen on that slope under the watchful eye of that deer while he held his position. That big buck had discovered a strategy for survival that worked and he stuck to it with a firmness that not even rifle shots could change.

In every case, a trophy buck has to beat the odds to survive. They have to adapt to the country in which they live. They have to come up with a strategy that helps them live long enough to grow big.

For the hunters who hope to bag a trophy deer, they have to learn to hunt smarter and use the tools available to them to get past a big buck's defenses. The smartness can be gained through your own experiences, the experiences of others and getting to know more about the deer themselves. As to the tools, there are proper clothes, guns, bows, camouflage, tree stands, scents and good binoculars and spotting scopes. And, of course, there is the deer call.

MULE DEER

Hiding Out in the Open

Most of the time, when we talk about deer being adaptable, we're talking about whitetails. They are the ones who can live successfully in the midst of man. They invade cities and suburbs. They can hide in the smallest wood lots. They thrive amid a wide variety of agricultural situations.

But mule deer shouldn't be shunned when it comes to variety, either. Everyone thinks about the majestic mule deer of the mountains. You've heard about it. It's a vision of a lofty buck above timberline, driven to the lowlands only by the coming of harsh winter. The truth of the matter, however, is that mule deer can also live in a wide range of environments. They survive in the semi-arid deserts of the Southwest. They inhabit the high plains of the North. You can find them in the foothills. And, of course, there are those high country bucks.

The key factor that seems to define mule deer habitat is a measure of seclusion. You can find them on the outskirts of the cities of the West or in the gardens of farmers and ranchers. They'll tolerate people then. But they come to those places only at feeding time, lured by the lush green forage. Once the feeding time is over, however, they want to be by themselves.

Mule deer seem to require that distance from man. They like their own place, where man may be only a rare or intermittent visitor. And if you look at their defense mechanisms, you'll understand why.

Their huge, cupped ears are perfect for gathering sounds. With ears shaped like that, they couldn't help but be sensitive to the tiniest of distant noises. Their eyes, too, seem to be attuned to spotting distant movements. While not as acute as the eyes of an antelope, they are able to detect danger at a distance. Their sense of smell, too, seems to be more than adequate to pick up the odors of predators.

Mule deer aren't like whitetails in temperament, either. Whitetails seem to rely more on stealth to survive. They'll use their senses to detect danger and then make the most of a small area to elude that threat. Perhaps they'll sit tight in dense cover. Perhaps they'll quietly circle around behind. In either case, they'll make their decision quickly.

Mule deer, on the other hand, will make their decisions more slowly. They'll often wait the longest of times after detecting danger at a distance before making any move to get away. They'll stand and look at a hunter. They'll stay in their beds as a coyote comes closer. Only then, when they're positively sure that danger won't leave them alone, will they make a move to get away. When that move comes, they'll often rely on great distance to protect themselves. If a whitetail can track his movement in feet and yards, then a mule deer often uses hundreds of yards or even miles when he decides to take off.

When you look at the long-range defense mechanisms of a mule deer and its penchant for putting long distances between itself and danger, it isn't surprising that mule deer can survive very well out in the wide open spaces of the prairie, foothills and semi-arid desert. Within those environ-

Mule deer will rely on any available cover or topography to hide.
Mark Henckel photo.

ments, they use whatever is available to them for cover. In fact, it has always amazed me at how little it takes to conceal a mule deer.

Gordon Eastman and I were shooting film of mule deer in Wyoming last year and located an amazing feeding situation. There was one field in a creek bottom where seventy-five bucks would come in to feed each evening. A majority of the bucks had over twenty-five-inch spreads. As I said, the scene was amazing with so many mature, wide-racked mule deer together in one single field.

Those bucks would feed and loaf in that field all night long, then take off in the morning to head back to their bedding areas. We followed them one day and located where the biggest group of them was bedding down. It turned out to be nothing more than a little swale in the hills with some sagebrush in it. But once they laid down in that sagebrush, the bucks all but disappeared. As I watched them through my binoculars and spotting scope, I told myself at the time

Mule Deer ■

that it would have been awfully easy to walk or drive right past the group. When they sat still, they blended in so well. Their coloration was right. The terrain offered just enough cover. If a buck or two hadn't gotten up from time to time to wander over to a new bedding spot, you'd never have seen them.

A patch of sagebrush, however, is more than enough to hide deer. So is a tall field of wheat during the summer. A rocky ridge will hold mule deer. And so will a dry creek bed. Almost any wrinkle in the land, patch of brush or cactus or even standing crop will provide mule deer with a place to hide.

So when you hunt mule deer in non-mountain environments, look for any aberrations in the land. Any break in the surroundings is likely to hold mule deer. If that break happens to be in a place where few people ever go, it's even more likely to hold mule deer. This is especially true during hours of full daylight. And when you find them, expect them to be bedded down and blending in well with their surroundings. Expect, too, that you may have to walk almighty close to them to get them out of their beds, too.

Frank Martin, a friend of mine from Lewistown, Montana, told me a bowhunting story once about how tight those mule deer can sit. He was walking slowly down a narrow little swale that had some water and brush in the bottom of it when he happened to glance out of the corner of his eye and see a mule deer buck in his bed just a few yards away that was watching him. Frank knew that if he stopped, the mule deer buck would get up and run away. In fact, if he even went through the motions of nocking and drawing an arrow that deer would be gone. So what he did was keep walking and circle back around the deer. When he completed the circle and was walking down the swale again, he was doing it with an arrow on his string and the bow at full draw. Once again, the bedded mule deer buck watched him come and was going to let him pass. It's too bad. The story would be so much better if Frank had hit the deer when he let go of the arrow. But unfortunately, a walking release isn't something that bowhunters usually practice. As a result, he missed the deer and the buck ran off. But the story does illustrate the staying power of a bedded mule deer buck who thinks the cover is hiding him. And the truth of the matter is that it almost worked. Frank just happened to spot him out of the corner of his eye.

This tendency to stay bedded makes spotting deer at any distance tough during daylight hours. At morning and evening, when the deer are feeding or on their way to and from feeding grounds, spotting open country deer becomes a lot easier. That's one reason why open-ground deer hunters often concentrate their efforts on morning and evening hunts and take a break during the middle of the day.

While mule deer can find all the ingredients of survival on the desert and prairie, you should know that they are more vulnerable there, both to hunting pressure and to pressures from the environment. Escape cover available to mountain mule deer is generally better than that which you find in non-mountain areas. Frankly, humans can't move through the high country with as much ease as they can move over flat ground or even foothill areas. Vast tracts of timber found in the mountains make it more difficult to find deer which have escaped. On the prairie or desert, there aren't as many options as hiding places. As a result, hunters can generally be more effective in taking deer from non-mountain areas.

As I said, the environment also comes into play more than in the relatively stable mountain areas where food, water and cover are available in most years. Prairie deer tend to suffer more from boom and bust cycles. If you have a series of wet years with good food and water, deer numbers can grow rapidly. A series of mild winters will also contribute to a boom in deer numbers as all fat does drop twins or even triplets each spring. When the conditions are right, the population can multiply quickly.

On the other end of the spectrum, deer numbers can tumble fast, too. Because cover is so much at a premium, severe winters can really hit prairie deer hard. When the winters are long and cold and the snows pile deep, mortality rates can reach ninety percent or more in some areas. Drought conditions can also hold deer numbers down as available food supplies and watering areas disappear. Put drought summers and tough winters together and the situation can be extremely deadly.

This boom and bust cycle means that in general, prairie mule deer herds in places like Montana, Wyoming, Idaho and Colorado could vary a great deal from year to year. It also means that mule deer probably won't be able to count on the same longevity that mountain deer enjoy. A biologist once told me that prairie fawns stand a much better chance of surviving their first winter than mountain fawns do simply because the mountain fawns have to cope with tougher winters every year. But get past that first winter and mountain deer stand a much better chance of living to old age. The prairie deer are more likely to be victims of the first tough winter.

All of these factors come into play if you have a choice to make—when and where you're going to hunt or even when and where you're going to photograph deer. If given the choice, you'll know that a series of mild winters and wet summers will produce the best deer numbers in non-mountain areas. If drought and tough winters have happened recently, perhaps you'd be better off to look for mule deer in the mountains. The same factors come into play if you're looking for a trophy buck. The key question here would be how long it has been since tough environmental conditions laid the population low. If it has been within the past three or four years, truly big bucks might be few and far between.

In like manner, you should take a look at the type of country you plan to hunt. How much security cover does it have? Areas of extensive badlands, rugged hills, scattered timber or deep cuts are likely to hold more possibilities for mule deer than acre after acre of unbroken flat ground. You should also ask how much human traffic is using the area both in and out of hunting season. As I said, mule deer like their solitude. And if there is little cover and much hunting pressure, it's very likely that the deer that are in the area

Mule deer can find the ingredients of life even on the desert or prairie.
Frank R. Martin photo.

will never get a chance to grow very old.

The ideal situation for open-ground mule deer would be ample cover, a number of years of good weather conditions and little human traffic at any time of the year. Given a situation like that, you'd be amazed how many mule deer the prairie or semi-arid desert can produce. And at morning and dusk, you'll be amazed at how many you can see.

Mountain Muleys

Mule deer of the prairie are much like the grasses that grow there. They flourish in the good times. They wither in the bad. In much the same way, mule deer of the mountains are like the mountains themselves. They're solid. They're enduring. And rather than show the effects of just one or two years, their very existence is chiseled in the passage of time.

Mountain mule deer are steeped in tradition. In their world, they must endure the rigors of drastic seasonal changes every year. They must adapt their lives to making the most of the benefits of these seasonal changes. They must adapt their lives to avoiding the harsh realities of the bad times.

Put in simple terms, they go up the mountains in summer. They come back down to spend the winter. Done correctly, they can enjoy the lush forage that summer rains bring to the high country. They can avoid the deep snow of the mountaintops and feed on the valley floors in winter. But the arrangement is anything but simple.

Instead, mountain muleys have to rely on the knowledge gained by their predecessors to survive. They learn traditions passed from one generation to the next. To do anything else is almost sure death at the hands of a high country winter.

How complicated are the traditions? Let's look at some examples.

In the Stillwater River valley of Montana, there exists a winter range that attracts several thousand deer each winter. For one thing, the valley is at lower elevation than the nearby Beartooth Mountains. For another, there's a wind belt that blows down the valley which keeps the ridges clear and melts off the snow whenever the warm winds blow. I'm sure that in the past, everyone just figured the deer that inhabited the valley each winter were from the mountains. But in more recent times, radio collars and coded neckbands were fitted on the deer to try to determine where these animals spent the summer. Surprisingly, some of the same deer that are seen on this range in winter spend the summer months near Tower Junction in Yellowstone National Park. These deer aren't from the Beartooths. This group of deer is actually from the other side of the Beartooths. Yet back they come every winter, hiking the forty-or-more miles over the highest mountain range in Montana. And each spring, they hike back.

The mule deer of the Bridger Range, near Bozeman, offer a similar view, based on the work done by Dave Pac and others in the Montana Department of Fish, Wildlife and Parks. Pac found that the mule deer of the Bridgers were actually broken down into a number of well-defined herd units. Each unit had a specific summer range and a specific winter range which they would inhabit in specific seasons. Some east side herd units would winter on the east side of the mountains. Others would migrate to the west side. And not only were they tied to these specific areas in specific seasons, he found he could even predict when they'd make their moves back and forth. All it took was the first skiff of snow in September to trigger the migrations of deer that had to cross the high divide between one side of the mountains and the other. Deer that didn't have to cross the divide might not even budge through the early snows. It might take a foot or even two feet of snow before they'd start to move. But in either case, the triggering mechanism for the herd units was uniform and predictable, based on the traditions passed onto those deer by their predecessors.

How could such an intricate and predictable system be worked out by the deer? It's a simple case of traditions that survived. Deer that broke with those traditions and did something else probably perished in the process. They didn't live to pass on the failed traditions. Those deer who successfully solved the migration puzzles were able to pass on successful traditions of survival for the deer which followed in their footsteps.

Another key ingredient of the migrations is the fact that mountain mule deer tend to be longer-lived than their counterparts on the prairie. While prairie deer tend to survive in great numbers only for as long as lush forage and mild winters allow them, the more reliable rainfall and security cover of the mountains tend to allow deer that survive their first year to grow to relatively ripe old ages. It's those older

Mule Deer

*Mule deer follow annual migration paths through the high country.
Jim Hamilton photo.*

does and bucks which will lead the way on the migrations. The younger ones just trail along and learn the paths.

When you know how the system works, you can see how fragile the arrangement really is. And, it can be fragile at both ends.

Suppose, for example, mule deer have traveled a migratory route for centuries that led them to a choice piece of winter range somewhere in the Rockies. But booming population from a nearby city or town, resort, mine or what-have-you brings civilization to the winter range. More than a few houses or summer homes begin to pop up on the winter range. Knowing the nature of mule deer, they'll tend to back off from the new level of activity. Back them off far enough and you could lose the winter range, the deer that wintered there and the tradition for muleys that spread out over a wide area of the mountains.

In the same way, heavy hunting pressure in the high country can put too great a stress on the deer there. If you wipe out the deer population of a particular drainage, or shoot off all the old bucks who know the migratory tradition, you could be ending the deer opportunities in that drainage for years and years until some new pioneers discover the tradition for themselves and pass it along.

If those sound like doom and gloom scenarios, in some ways they are. As tough and resilient as mule deer can be, you're dealing with some fragile arrangements here that have taken centuries to develop. More than anything, though, I guess what I'm trying to stress is the importance of moderation in our hunting the backcountry and the dire importance of preserving the winter ranges that mountain mule deer need to survive.

If the fragile nature of the migratory traditions are the down side of mountain mule deer, the up side is the long lives of the deer and the predictability of their movements. Whether you're a hunter or wildlife photographer or just someone who likes to watch deer, there isn't anything quite as impressive as a mountain muley.

Once you learn a migratory path, you can count on the deer walking that path at about the same time each fall. That means a person only has to pay close attention to weather patterns to determine when the most productive time is to be out there. It also means that big bucks which are beyond the reach of all but the horseback hunters early in the fall will come to you if you can hold out until late in the season.

One friend of mine does just that. While I spend the early

Deer will summer in the high country and winter down low.
Michael H. Francis photo.

season hiking the high country, he goes upland bird hunting, duck hunting and maybe chases an antelope. But as
soon as the snows start swirling, he heads to a particular
mountain drainage where he has dropped his buck every
year for the past 20. Invariably, the deer he drops is at least
a good four-point. He usually does it in anywhere from one
to three days of hunting. And, as a side benefit, he has snow
to help him on the drag back to his car. His arrangement is a
sweet one and it doesn't keep him from enjoying his hunting of other species every fall.

A side benefit of hunting the migration is that mule deer
bucks often are in the rut by that point of the season.
They're apt to make mistakes that they wouldn't make a
month earlier or a month later. I found out just how rut-
crazed those bucks could be in the last week of November a
few years ago.

I was hunting the edge of a winter range, glassing the
steep slopes of a mountain valley at dawn. What I spotted
first was a herd of elk, about a half-mile away and perhaps

500 feet of elevation away from me. There wasn't a bull in the bunch that I could see as it strung out and headed further up the slope. But that didn't mean there wasn't a bull nearby. With elk season running at the same time as deer season, I figured it was worth the steep uphill hike.

It took plenty of huffing, puffing and more than a few rest stops to climb that steep slope. Eventually, I broke out on a long and narrow bench about three-fourths of the way to the top with a big patch of aspens and scattered brush. My eyes were trained for elk as I walked through the aspen patch. But there were no elk to see. Instead, when I walked out the far side, I saw that I had pushed three deer out ahead of me. There was a doe, her fawn, and a nice four-point mule deer that was far more in love with that doe than he was frightened of me.

The three deer strung out until they stopped on a knob about 200 yards away, the buck following that doe step for step. With a standing shot like that, the buck should have been mine instantly. But it was one of those times when my marksmanship also decided to migrate. I stood there and missed four straight shots at that standing buck. I would have missed some more, but the gun only had four rounds in it at the time. By all rights, the buck should have run off. But the doe ran toward me about fifty yards and the buck followed. Rummaging through my pockets, I found another cartridge, chambered it and missed the buck again. Once again, the doe ran toward me about fifty yards and the buck followed. Digging past the candy bar and toilet paper, I found yet another cartridge. This time, at 100 yards, the buck dropped dead in his tracks, while the doe and fawn ran off never to be seen again.

The love interest of that buck certainly helped me. But I couldn't help but think that the migratory nature of that mountain buck was on my side as well. The mountains surrounding that mountain valley were extremely rugged. The slope I had climbed was extremely steep. It was possible that even though this was the last week of the season, I was the first hunter that the deer had encountered during the summer and fall. While a more hunter-wise buck might

Mule Deer ■

have dumped the doe and saved himself, this old buck was out of practice and simply forgot what to do.

Hunting the migratory paths of mountain mule deer is a good strategy. So is hunting areas slightly higher in elevation than the winter ranges. These tend to be staging areas where mule deer will often hang up until more snow and cold move them onto the winter range itself.

No matter how you plan to hunt them, you can see the key is knowledge of the traditions of the deer. You can catch them in the high country early. You can catch them on the migration paths after the snows begin. Or you can hunt them on or near the winter ranges. But to do any of those things, you have to know where the deer will be at particular times.

Just as the traditions of the deer take time to learn, a hunter can expect his own luck to get better and better as he puts in more and more seasons in the same hunting area. It takes time to learn the traditions of a mountain mule deer. You can put in that time yourself, hire a guide or outfitter who has put in the time or hunt with a friend who has put in the time and learned. But no matter which way you go, once you've learned those traditions well enough to capitalize on them, you'll have opened up an opportunity for yourself to see some of the biggest and best muleys that the West has to offer. And you'll be able to cash in on those traditions year, after year, after year.

You Can Get There from Here

Hunting was different in the old days. If you were lucky, you lived on a farm. You could use the farm truck. You could use the farm horse. With those tools, you could invade some of the far reaches of hunting country. But that wasn't the mainstream of hunting in the old days—not the way I remember it, not the way I've seen it in pictures and not the way I've been told about it.

No, the old days mostly meant the family sedan or station

wagon to carry you to hunting country. It meant two-wheel-drive, not four. It meant tire chains, not computer-drawn traction tires. It meant bulky clothing, bulky camping equipment and even bulky food. Were hunters tougher in the old days than they are today? I'd cast my vote in favor of those tough old birds. They had to be tough, just to survive the gear they had to tote.

The mule deer hunter of today has far more on his side when it comes to effectively penetrating the hideaways of the big mule deer bucks. In almost every facet of the sport, improvements have made things smaller, lighter, stronger and more convenient to use.

If you don't believe it, just look at the hunting camps of today. In the old days, you may have had a wall tent. There are some wall tents in use today, too. But there are travel trailers, lightweight nylon tents and tent trailers, too. Look at sleeping gear. In the old days, you mostly had wool blankets or sleeping bags made of wool or heavy batting or possibly goose down. Today, you've got your choice of goose down or a variety of synthetic fibers that are even better than goose down because they're just as light and will keep you warm even when you're wet. Cooking over an open fire has been replaced by a variety of propane, white gas or unleaded gas stoves and the thin-gauge steel Simms stoves which burn wood and can keep a wall tent warm in the coldest of weather. Packing food into your camp invariably meant canned goods and bulk in the old days. Today, with freeze-dried meals, pastas, rice and potatoes and vacuum packaging for meats, you can literally eat better in camp than you do at home.

But if there's one revolution that has really changed hunting for deer, elk and everything else, it's the new developments in vehicles. If you really wanted to get into the backcountry in the old days, most hunters had two-wheel-drive-and-chains or four-legs-and-hay horsepower. Now, hunters can buy four-wheel-drive vehicles of all shapes and sizes. Motor bikes and snowmobiles power you past the end of the road. In areas where motorized vehicles aren't allowed, there are hunters using mountain bikes effectively

Mule Deer ∎

Hunters on horseback can reach some of the more remote deer areas.
Mark Henckel photo.

to get back into areas where only horses went before. And if you prefer to walk, there are lightweight backpacking tents, sleeping bags, stoves, cooking untensils and even clothing that will allow you to carry a complete camp on your back.

If you add in the number of hunters in the field today, you've got a situation where almost every available corner of mule deer country is feeling the tread of hunters' boots at some time during the season. Well, almost all of them are. And that's the challenge.

If you look hard enough, you can still find the places that few, or even no, hunters ever reach. It's in these places where the big bucks often hide. It's in these places where you can find the solitude that brings most hunters to mule deer country in the first place.

How do you find them? There are several ways.

The first way, and probably the easiest way, you can find solitude is to pay for it. Fee hunting on private ground is the latest rage in the West. If you're willing to pay enough for it often in the hundreds of dollars—you can get exclusive or nearly exclusive use of a piece of private ground for a few days. If you're willing to pay enough to an outfitter—often a thousand or a few thousand dollars—you'll get your solitude, your meals and your lodging and a guide to go along and help you find the big bucks in the course of a five-day, seven-day or nine-day hunt.

Another way to find that solitude is to do your homework with public land maps and topographic maps, searching for the hidey holes that are far away from the roads. You can look for rugged country to protect you. You can look for desolate stretches far between towns. You can look for wilderness areas or big blocks of national forest land. Then you have to figure out how to penetrate those areas with four-wheeled or four-legged horsepower, two-wheel motor or pedal power or with the strength of your legs.

Or, you might get lucky. If you happen to live in the West and are truly blessed with landowner friends, perhaps they'll let you hunt on their places. If you happen to have hunting friends who have been in an area before, you can plumb the depths of their knowledge and learn some hunting spots. Or, if you're truly lucky, you'll marry the only daughter of a rancher who owns a huge place crawling with mule deer. But how many of us can get that lucky?

From my own experience, I can tell you that these hiding places for mule deer are almost invariably in the roughest country. I got my lesson in that early in life when I was hunting the Crazy Mountains of Montana. In those rugged mountains, we invariably found the bucks on the upper third of the slopes where patches of scrub juniper hung on amid the shale rock, scattered timber and patches of grass.

One time, we were hunting a spot where a lightning-caused fire had burned off a lot of the available timber. I suppose every mountain range has a spot they simply call "The Burn." This one was ours.

On the way up there, we were walking up a creek bottom and heard a tremendous rockslide at the head of the canyon. At the sound of the commotion, we scrambled to a spot

Mule Deer ■

Gordon Eastman uses an all-terrain vehicle to pack out a buck.
Don Laubach photo.

where we could see what was going on. We could see the shale rocks still coming down. It was a big slide that seemed to generate from one small spot. That piqued our curiosity, so we walked over to the slide.

What we found were two two-point mule deer bucks buried amid the rubble. Perhaps they were trying to scratch out an existence in that rocky country and just got caught in the slide. But I've always figured that they probably started it when one or both of them lost their footing on that steep and precarious slope. In any event, that rockslide was the end of them. They had been trapped in that slide, apparently all the way down the mountain. Their hides had been completely pulled off their bodies and up over their heads, just as if someone had skinned them.

That made an early impression on me as to just how rough and tough the country can be that these deer inhabit. It also made a point to me that one false step by anyone in that harsh land can mean the end of them, too. It's difficult country where you learn to be sure-footed or you can die. It's certainly not a place where the faint of heart should be hunting. Yet that's where the deer live.

Another key ingredient in finding a mule deer hidey hole is to make sure it has all the things that deer need to survive. Every hunter knows those basics. They are food, water and a secure place to hide. But sometimes, there's another factor at work.

Dick Hosford, for example, ranches on the Tongue River in the heart of a mule deer area that includes both river bottom pastures and some rugged, pine-covered hills. Dick will tell you that you can find anywhere from 100 to 200 mule deer in the bottoms in the early morning or at dusk. But during two weeks of hunting last fall, we never saw any of the big bucks there.

Instead, you had to head back into those rugged hills to find the bigger bucks. You might not see five or ten deer there in the course of a day. But you stood a much better chance of finding a good one. To his way of thinking, the reason for that was that we were hunting there in the early stages of the rut. At night, the big bucks would come to the bottoms. They'd key in on a receptive doe. And that doe would lead the buck on something of a wild goose chase before she'd allow him to breed her. That wild goose chase took place back in those hills. Whether that was the actual reason or not, I don't know. But I can hardly fault Dick's logic. I shot a big four-by-four muley there last fall and we found him and every other big deer far off the river, back in those hills.

All I can say is that those hills were the hiding spot for the bigger bucks. We could have shot as many does or little bucks as we wanted on the river. But Dick's knowledge pointed out the place where the big bucks were found. And that's all that it takes to discover a hidey hole.

One final consideration that should be mentioned is that land features can create hiding spots for both mule deer and whitetails. In river systems, look to the islands that require boat or canoe travel to reach them as good places for whitetails to hide. For mule deer, look to streams that must be crossed, steep slopes that must be climbed, or even long walks that must be made through unproductive country before you get to a place that can hold deer.

One example I can offer was a hunting spot I had along the Gallatin River. This blue-ribbon trout stream rushes cold and fast and sometimes treacherous through the mountains before it becomes one of the headwater streams of the Missouri. A well-traveled state highway follows the river along most of its passage through those mountains.

What I found is that few hunters ever try to cross the river, except at places where they could find a road or a bridge. As a result, there was very little hunting pressure on the far side of the river and there were some good mule deer bucks over there.

Our hunting strategy involved taking our wading boots along with our hiking boots. We'd wade the river, then stash the wading boots on the far side. We'd pull on our hiking boots and begin climbing the mountains on the far side.

Hunting that country wasn't easy. The slopes were steep that led to the hiding spots for the mule deer bucks. But that steep country turned out to be a friend when you shot your deer over there. The slope was so steep that it would be relatively easy to skid the deer back to the river. Floating a deer across the Gallatin was also easy. The hardest part was wading the river and hiking up the slopes in the first place.

Over the years, I've taken three twenty-five-inch-wide or better mule deer bucks out of that spot. They were always on the high ground at the end of the steep climb. But the bucks were always big enough that they made the work of getting there more than worthwhile.

One of the keys to finding places like that one is to use your maps well. Study the lay of the land. Look for the places that other hunters miss. Look for the places that take just a bit more ingenuity and drive to reach. Look for the ingredients within that spot that will provide for all the needs of the deer that live there. Then look for a way to get there.

With all the tools available to the hunters of today, there are few places that a hunter can't reach if he really wants to hunt them. It's true. You can get there from here. And once you get there, you just might find the mule deer buck of your dreams.

Offense and Defense

Hunting for mule deer can sometimes be strange. And a hunter had better be prepared for that.

Consider, for a moment, the defensive tendencies of mule deer. Almost any hunter who has spent much time going after them will tell you that they'll very often give you a second shot. Whitetail hunters aren't generally prepared for that. But almost invariably with mule deer, and young mule deer especially, you'll spook them only to have them run out a couple of hundred yards, then turn broadside and look back at you. For that reason, seasoned mule deer hunters are always prepared, even if they miss the first time around.

Behavioralists will tell you that the reason mule deer will often stop and turn is to identify the source of the danger. Rather than the run first, run fast, worry-about-the-danger-later nature of whitetails, mule deer are more deliberate in their actions. They evolved against such natural enemies as the wolf, coyote, mountain lion and grizzly bear. Knowing what they were up against was undoubtedly a defensive trait that survived evolution. And, if you think about it, that trait served them well against their predators until they came up against a predator that could reach out 200 or 300 yards and knock them down.

Just so you don't get the impression that every mule deer will stop and turn, however, you should know that it doesn't always work. Big bucks, especially big bucks who have been shot at and missed when they stopped and turned, will often just keep running. Mule deer in the timber will often put enough distance between you and them that even if they do stop, there are going to be trees in the way so you can't see them. And some hunters maintain that the evolution of mule deer is continuing and by process of natural selection—shooting off the ones that stop and turn—that we're coming up with a new trait to keep running until they're out of sight.

While mule deer have always had the tendency to stop and turn, blowing the half-distress call will only enhance your chances of making that stop come within rifle range. The key is to blow it just loud enough so that a running deer can hear it. What I like to do is blow it with increasing volume until I get a reaction from the deer. And, of course, I have my gun or camera ready to take advantage of the situation when the deer does stop.

Another defensive weapon that mule deer often use is to sit tight and wait for danger to pass. Among members of the deer family, that isn't so different. Whitetails will do the same thing. But I doubt that whitetails do it with the same tenacity.

Let me give you an example from the past. I was hunting with my son on a ranch north of Miles City, driving a four-wheel drive down a ranch trail that bordered a field of tall grass. It was just before sunset on a cloudy, gloomy day. It was still legal shooting time, but the gloom was making for a low-light hunting situation. About 250 yards out in the field, I saw a deer standing up with just the top half of its head sticking above the grass. Glassing it through my binoculars, I could see that it was a buck. That was good enough for my son, so he stepped out of the vehicle, took a steady rest and, after I told him to aim for the head, he touched off a shot. The deer still stood there, apparently unfazed by his effort.

While my son is a good shot, I figured that cutting the distance would only improve his chances, so I told him to get closer. He cut the distance to about 125 yards and the buck still stood there, so I told him to shoot again. This time, I

Mule deer will try to identify danger before they decide to run.
Bob Zellar photo.

heard the bullet hit, but it sounded like the boy hit an antler. Sure enough, the buck went down and came back up
again, bounding dead away from him. So I told him to shoot
again. This time, I could see the deer swing down and sit
there, hit solidly in the spine. As we ran together toward the
buck to finish him off, I mentally told myself that the buck
looked like a good one, better than I'd first thought. But

then the light was a little off and he was quite a ways out there when I first spotted him.

It was only after I ran past the first buck—shot in the skull square between the eyes—that I realized this deer we were running toward was a better buck, a second buck we had never seen before. The first buck was a two-year-old two-by-two with his antlers tall and wide for his age. The second was a three-year-old three-by-three with a rack nearly two feet wide and two feet high. In that light, they were close enough in appearance that a four-power rifle scope would hardly tell the difference. With tags for both deer, the animals were far from wasted. But it still amazed me that the big buck would have such staying power. That buck had stayed in its bed through the approach of our vehicle. It had stayed there through my son's first missed shot, a healthy blast from a .270 caliber rifle. And it hadn't gotten up until the smaller buck must have all but fallen on him after being shot itself. Then, and only then, did the bigger buck get up to flee.

The experience taught me some things about mule deer and provided a good lesson for my son. It reinforced the lesson that you have to make positive sure about your target, even when you're already sure about it. And it made us both wonder about the fix we could have been in had there not been a legal tag for each of the bucks.

Finally, it reinforced an old lesson for me about following up your shots after you take them. Mule deer, and whitetails, too, for that matter, are tough animals. Even with the force and speed of today's rifle calibers, you can't always tell that you've made a good shot.

I can remember a hunt of almost 20 years ago on another eastern Montana ranch when a friend and I walked toward a small patch of brush nestled at the base of an open ridge. It was late in the season and my friend, Jack Tanner, had told me earlier that all he wanted was some meat to hang his two tags on. If he saw a buck, fine. If he saw a doe, that was fine, too.

As we walked closer to the patch of brush, it erupted with

Mule deer are both big and tough. They have to be to survive.
Michael H. Francis photo.

deer. There were does and fawns running everywhere. Jack was shooting an old .25-35 with a peep sight and first swung on a deer running straight away from him up the ridge. After firing a shot in that direction with apparently no effect, he saw another deer that was closer and running off toward the right. He swung on that deer, shot and watched it tumble.

"Well, I got one," he hollered over with pride. "No," I responded. "You got two."

While Jack had been shooting at the second deer, the first one had suddenly reared up on its hind legs and tumbled backward down the hill. He had made a fatal lung shot on the doe, but its strength had allowed it to run another forty or fifty yards before it finally piled up. Certainly, the country we were hunting was open enough that Jack probably would have seen the deer when he walked up the ridge to get the second doe. But it made me wonder about what would have happened had we been hunting in the timber. Another forty or fifty yards could have carried that deer out of sight.

A walk over to the scene showed us that following up the shot would have made the question of whether or not he hit it easy to answer. From the point of impact, the doe had left a strong blood trail all the way up the ridge to the point where it finally tumbled backward.

But how many rifle hunters, often taking shots at deer that are 200 or 300 yards away, will take the time to walk over and check on their shot? Some will. Others will just pass it off as a miss and walk away.

That isn't the only time that I've had mule deer run after being hit, either. On the same ranch, I had a heart-shot mule deer run for over 100 yards and out of sight before he tipped over. As I recall, I was lamenting loud and long about my poor shooting exhibition on that deer when Jack walked over, found the blood trail and then found the deer.

Mule deer are big and strong. They have to be to survive in the harsh climate of the West. That's one of the defenses they've developed over the centuries. And even if you're shooting a big caliber gun to take them, you have to be ready to follow your shot.

One last story should illustrate just how tough they can be. It involved a two-point mule deer buck that a woman at work shot as the first deer of her life. It was a deer that she earned the hard way, having learned to be just a little gun-shy in addition to suffering from a healthy case of buck fever.

First, she missed a couple of bucks with more than a couple of shots. Then, she sustained a half-circle cut above her eye when the recoil of the .243 caliber rifle drove the scope into her forehead. Finally, we found another buck for her. Her first shot kicked up dust halfway between us and the deer. The second shot kicked up dust closer to the animal. The third shot put the animal down.

Running over there with her, I volunteered to hold her gun while she cut out her tag and bubbled with excitement over her first Montana deer. But even as she bubbled, I watched the deer's eye change from cloudy to clear. I handed the gun back to her just as the buck got back onto its feet and ran away. Again she hit the deer and put it down. The bubbling continued until the deer got up a second time and she had to shoot it again. This time, it didn't get up.

In field dressing the deer, I can tell you that all three shots were in the chest. I don't know how that deer kept getting up. But as I said, mule deer are tough.

You can take them with a rifle like a .243, a .25-35, a .270 or anything else, but be prepared for the unexpected. Just when you're sure you've got them down and you've overcome their defenses, they'll come up with an offense that will surprise you.

WHITETAILS

Deer in the Timber

White-tailed deer in the timber can be such a puzzlement, especially for hunters who hail from the wide-open West. In the West, you grow accustomed to putting binoculars and spotting scopes to good use. You can see a long way and spot deer at a distance, using your optics to glass distant mountain slopes or scan the prairies. Once you spot them, then you figure out a way to get closer, using the lay of the land to help you stalk your prey.

Whitetails in the timber are different. Distance isn't the problem here. Stalking isn't necessarily the best tactic. And high-powered optics aren't always needed.

But two things are basically the same, no matter where you happen to be. One of them is the deer. The other is the deer's need to use the land. And it's in putting these two factors together that a hunter finds success whether he's hunting the East, the West or anywhere in between.

Whitetails in the timber need food, water and cover. Even more than mule deer, they need safe travel paths in between the three places that provide those necessities of life. And just like all deer, they follow patterns that dictate their daily activities.

To learn the daily patterns and the paths that the deer follow, you have to go into the deer woods before the season starts, during the season and after the season and learn to read the signs that the deer leave behind.

Over a number of years, I spent a lot of time walking the deer trails in a big oak forest in the upper Midwest. I'll admit that when I first started walking them, they seemed to follow no rhyme nor reason. They were simply a maze that might lead up one ridge, down another and across a broad valley.

But as I walked them more and more, I began to realize some things. Even in a big forest that looks pretty much the same at first, there are some subtle differences in the land. There might be a ridge where the brush is just a little tighter than elsewhere and that forms a bedding area. Instead of following a path to food that's visible for a long distance, there's a path that leads down a narrow little valley where the deer are more hidden.

I learned there were main trails and secondary trails and seldom-used trails. Each served their purpose, some before the hunting season and some during it.

But where do you start in trying to learn these things?

The most obvious way is to study the landforms within the forest. There might be a swamp. There could be a creek. Or there might be brushy draws or fingers of heavy timber or long ridges. Any or all of these landforms can affect the way the deer use the land.

If there's a creek, a deer trail will almost surely parallel it. A swamp that few humans penetrate might form a secure bedding area, even during the height of the hunting season. Whitetails will follow brushy draws, fingers of heavy timber and long ridges in moving from one place to another. And just because you see does and fawns using a trail, that

When hunting big areas of timber, find the travel routes deer favor.
Mark Henckel photo.

doesn't necessarily mean bucks will be using it.

I can remember one situation when my hunting partners and I detected what turned out to be pretty much a bucks-only pattern in that oak forest we hunted. To the west of us, there was a long, deep and relatively open basin where someone could see a deer for a half-mile or more. Does would move through that basin whenever the pressure was on during the hunting season. But you never saw a buck there.

What we discovered is that the bucks would skirt the big basin, sneaking through the tiny swales and valleys that bordered it. The oaks were a little younger and thicker in those swales and you couldn't see as far. The deer trails that cut through the area weren't pounded as hard as others that cut through the big basin. Sometimes, they were hardly distinguishable as trails at all. But it was in those swales where we built our tree-bark sets and settled down to sit with our backs to big oak trees for opening day.

For a number of years, those stands worked like magic on opening morning. We'd hike in to them in the dark and be settled in quietly long before shooting time arrived. By the time the other hunters began working the big oak woods, we'd be waiting. I missed two whitetail bucks on successive years on opening morning and bagged a nice whitetail, a small eight-point, eastern count whitetail buck while shooting a twelve-gauge slug gun fitted with a peep sight. One of my partners never missed as he bagged big-bodied, acorn-fed bucks that inhabited those woods. And the other partner took the biggest one of all, a gnarly-horned eleven-point that dressed out at over 200 pounds.

All this happened in the years before tree stands became popular. If we hunted those woods today, a tree stand would probably be very much a part of our arsenal. After all, the other factors are very likely still the same. The bucks probably still sneak through the cover near the big basin rather than exposing themselves by running right through it. And I'm sure there are still plenty of other hunters there, pushing the deer as they walk around.

In my hunting out West today, my strategy for taking whitetails is still very much the same. There generally aren't as many other hunters here to move the deer around. But when I do get into situations with other hunters, I always try to use their movements to my benefit. I do that by trying to read the landforms and picking out the places where deer are likely to go when pushed by others.

I'll admit it right here and now—I've never been a big fan of organized deer drives. Even though I know they're effective in moving deer toward waiting hunters, to me they always seem very much like an accident waiting to happen. You have a line of hunters carrying guns and people on stand at the end and the deer squeezed in between. They can only be as safe as the people involved in the driving and standing. And it can only be as safe as those people in an excited condition when they spot those deer in between.

Given the choice, I'll take the informal drives of other hunters doing their own hunting and me trying to figure out safe spots where the deer might be pushed.

Another effective method of taking advantage of deer that are bumped by moving hunters is more of a variation on a tactic that I use for elk. In the elk situation, what you do is have one hunter walk about fifty or seventy-five yards ahead of another hunter. The trailing hunter either follows the same path or is located slightly higher up the slope. In either case, both hunters move slowly through the woods.

Often, a white-tailed deer will wait until the first hunter passes before getting up out of his bed. Other times, the deer will circle around to the side of the first hunter. In either case, the trailing hunter has the opportunity to see the deer. And in both cases, the deer is likely to have his attention focused on the first hunter to pass through.

If you happen to be trying to walk up a whitetail on your own, the key is to make sure you do your walking slowly. Just find a patch of cover where the deer will be bedded or will be moving through and take all the time in the world in working your way through it. Take a step or two or three, stop for several minutes, then move on slowly. This way, you can see deer that might be on their feet and moving toward you. You also will make deer that are trying to wait for you to pass so nervous that they may get up out of their beds. And it will give you the opportunity to really look over the cover as you walk. This is one time where some good optics can actually help a whitetail hunter, even in the thickest of woods. Using binoculars to scan the brush or timber will force you to concentrate your eyesight on a single spot. When concentrating that way, you can pick out the twitch of an ear or the shine off an antler. You might see only parts of a deer through the thick brush that will give their position away.

Finally, look for the feeding areas, either in the woods itself or on the fringes of the timber. Deer will pattern to these places, usually at morning or evening. You can scout these places before the season begins to determine the deer movements and what deer are available. Then you can plan your ambush either at the feeding grounds themselves or on the trails that lead to and from the feeding grounds.

Whitetails will often move through narrow paths of cover.
Frank R. Martin photo.

As I said before, the deer themselves are the same and so are their needs. Whitetails will make the most of available food, cover and water. They'll follow paths to reach these places. And they'll walk those paths at the same times each day until something disrupts their pattern.

All you have to do is put in the time to learn the places

where whitetails roam and to look at the ways the deer will use the landforms within a patch of timber. Once you figure those things out, you can put yourself in line for consistent success, while others are still walking aimlessly through the woods.

Farm Country Bucks

Some of my most pleasant evenings have been spent in farm country hunting whitetails. The time? Make it the first week of November. The place? Let it be a cutover barley field. The deer? Count them in the dozens.

Sitting with my back against a tree on the edge of the timber and with a camouflage net stretched in front of me, I've watched those whitetails for hours. Invariably, the first arrivals are the does with twin fawns. The first trio will arrive in a somewhat tentative fashion. They'll peek out of the brush, glance sideways in a nervous pattern, then walk carefully out into the barley stubble and begin feeding. Once they're established in the field, however, the parade of other does and fawns will begin in earnest. Small bucks will follow the parade, a bit more cautious, but still intent on filling stomaches that haven't been tended to since morning.

The scene in the field is always a delight. Does will feed contentedly. Fawns will alternately feed and play. Young bucks will test their power in mock fights, pushing and shoving against each others' spindly antlers. If you're patient and can keep the deer far enough away that you don't spook them by your presence, the big bucks will finally come. They'll be the most cautious of all. They'll tarry back in the brush. They'll peer out on the scene for long periods of time, then may decide to head back into the brush. Just as the light begins to fade, the big boys will finally decide to join the scene.

If you're a big buck hunter, it's that last half-hour of shooting light which is most precious of all. Unless you have the rut on your side and the bucks are careless, they'll

Bucks will bed in cover during daylight and feed in the open at night.
Michael H. Francis photo.

hold off at least until that precious thirty minutes before showing themselves. If you're lucky, one will emerge before shooting time ends for the day.

But even if one doesn't show up, the evening whitetail show is truly spectacular. At times, when the shooting day ended, I've wanted to stand up and applaud.

The thing about that evening show is that it always amazes me how many deer sometimes appear. If you walked the patches of timber and beat the brush through that country all day, you'd never see that many any other way.

Yet farm ground and whitetails go hand-in-hand from one end of the country to the other. The available food may differ from corn to wheat to barley to alfalfa. But farm crops have proven to be a boon for growing whitetails.

Hunting methods for the various types of farm ground differ. With the stubble field that I hunt, the evening stand is a deadly way to hunt. In that area, there is a mixture of tight brush and timber for bedding. There is the fallen grain for food. Water is available in several creeks. What I hunt is the evening destination of the deer. Daytime bedding areas are too available and too tough to consistently take deer from them.

I have a friend, however, who hunts the giant stubble fields of the Dakotas. Here, the wheat stubble is everywhere and it isn't possible to guess where an evening destination might be. It could be anywhere. The friend, instead, keys his hunting efforts squarely on the bedding areas.

There are far fewer spots where a whitetail can hide the day away. He pushes the tiny patches of brush and the shelter belts. He'll glass the rockpiles that farmers often create when they pick rocks out of their fields and stack them. He'll look for the tiny sloughs, marshes and ponds which have tall grass and reeds and cattails where deer will bed for the day.

In his country, the bedding areas are the weakest links in the daily lifestyles of the deer. They are the places where he can most predictably find them. So he'll work them religiously while basically ignoring the feeding areas.

While a deer stands out in the stubble, a deer in standing grain or corn is something else. Deer will walk into those fields and seem to vanish. Often they can feed and bed in the same spot and never step out where you can get a look at them.

I heard a hunting expert tell someone once that the only way to effectively hunt a field of standing corn was to mow it, burn it or plow it under. That would open it up so you could see the deer and hunt it effectively. Perhaps, but the farmer is going to frown on the practice.

While those are certainly ways to tackle a field of standing corn, I've heard of a better one. It was a solution created by a friend who liked to hunt white-tailed deer and pheasants alone. What he would do is stalk the game in those fields, going crosswise to the rows. Rather than walk the length of them like most hunters do, he would start near one end of the field and begin sneaking across the width of them.

He'd wear quiet clothing. He'd walk extremely slowly. And he'd poke his head through the standing corn a row at

Crops that whitetails favor will vary in different parts of the country.
Frank R. Martin photo.

a time. Looking low so he could see beneath the bulk of the foliage between the rows, he'd scan right and left in the furrow for as far as he could see to spot a snoozing pheasant or a sleeping buck. If nothing was hiding in that furrow, he'd quietly step into it and repeat the process by poking his head through the corn to look into the next furrow.

The hunter would cut a swath across the field that way, then move up the field a distance and cut another swath across. If the wind was blowing a bit and rattling the leaves on the corn, that made it so much better because it helped to mask the few sounds he was making himself. If no wind was blowing, he'd just have to be as quiet as he could.

The friend said he slipped in unnoticed on a lot of deer and pheasants that way. If everything worked right, they never knew he was coming. Yet to the best of his knowledge, few other hunters ever tried the trick themselves. The others always figured you needed plenty of people and had to form extensive drives that went the length of the rows.

Had the whitetails been on their feet and moving, it would have been more difficult to pin them down. Because they were bedded and many were napping in the corn field, it was much easier to cover a field completely.

That's the key to farm ground whitetails—locating the weak link and being able to pin them down to a particular pattern. Unless you're in a rut situation, that means studying the whitetails in your area and figuring out the daily routine. If it is the rut, there may be a certain travel route that the deer favor. It might be a narrow patch of brush between farm fields that leads from one big patch of cover to another. It might be a particular creek that offers them concealment, rather than exposing themselves in the fields.

In much of the West, it's the creek bottoms that define whitetail territory. The tangles of willow, Russian olive, wild rose and other cover species are where the deer concentrate during most of the hunting hours of the day.

I've had some good luck with a deer call in these areas during most hours of the day. One memorable afternoon, for example, shouldn't have been nearly as good as it was. All I was doing was walking a creek bottom to see what was hiding there.

The day was warm. The patch of cover wasn't exceptionally large. All it really had going for it was the brush that clung to the creek bottom and an old beaver channel which had started to flood the bottoms before the farmer dynamited the dam.

I followed a cattle trail into the part of the bottoms that was thick with willows. I'd make a common doe sound, then stop, walk a bit, call and stop again.

It's common knowledge that a whitetail buck will often hold in thick cover and let you walk past him. A ten-point, eastern-count buck tried to do just that. He let me walk within ten feet of where he was bedded before he bolted and snorted back at me. I'll admit it. The buck scared the daylights out of me. When I recovered my composure, I started walking and calling and stopping again. I hadn't gone twenty feet however before I glanced over to my right and there the buck was, just forty yards away. He had circled back and was coming in to the call. I froze and kept calling to him. Eventually, the buck disappeared into the brush again only to reappear at sixty yards out in the open.

Eventually, I walked over to the beaver dam and gave a couple more common doe sounds. Looking through my binoculars, I could see deer moving in the brush again. It was a different whitetail buck. Off to the right of that buck was another buck, this one a really big whitetail. As I stayed there and called, the two bucks just milled around in the brush.

Once again, I got up and started walking, seeing if I could get a little closer. I hadn't gone twenty-five feet when two more bucks leaped out of their beds, a six-point and an eight-point. These two started running toward the first two and those bucks also spooked. When I hit the half-distress call, however, all four bucks skidded to a stop. With more common doe sounds, they'd all mill around. They wouldn't come closer. They wouldn't leave. All four bucks were within seventy-five yards of me.

It was quite an afternoon. All those bucks so close. All of them either coming to the call, being stopped by the call or being held by the call.

Later in the week, we went through the area again and jumped does in addition to the bucks. It was just a prime bedding area for whitetails where they liked to hide during the middle of the day. I'm sure I could go back there again next year and find the situation hasn't changed.

For that area, this was the weak link in the whitetails' lifestyle. They made the most of agriculture for their food. They made the most of the cover that was available for their hiding spot. By keying in on the right area and the right time of day where whitetails concentrated and where I knew I could find them, I'd uncovered a farm ground pattern that may vary a bit in terms of crops and cover from one part of the country to the next, but is guaranteed to produce deer no matter where you put it to use.

On the Ground, in the Air

There's a hunting partner of mine who is a true, true believer in the power of the tree stand. He'll clamp a tree stand into a trunk so small that he bobs and weaves in even the slightest of breezes. He'll go higher, higher and higher in his quest to improve his view of the ground below and elude the eyes, ears and noses of the deer. And he'll tough it out up there in all kinds of weather from early in the season until late.

He's such a die-hard tree stand hunter that I like to tease him about it.

"Tree stand again, huh?"

"Yeah, I've got a good one."

"You know what they say about those trees."

"Great for whitetails, right?"

"Not exactly. What I've always heard is that the trees are only for the squirrels and nuts."

While I have my fun with him, it's hard to dispute the successes that tree stand hunters have amassed over the years. I'm not so certain anymore that the notion that deer never look up holds as true today as it once did. There are so many hunters in the trees in the whitetail woods that some deer have gotten wise to them.

It's not that all deer will scan the skies every moment of the day. But a wise old buck that's escaped a tree stand situation or has been the target of an ill-fated ambush in a particular spot will learn from his experiences. I've had old tree stand hunters tell me that you've got to be a lot more motionless in your stand than you had to be years ago. And increased hunting pressure everywhere has made deer more aware that strange noises and strange sights are things for whitetails to avoid.

As for their applications with a deer call, that also has received some mixed reviews among hunters who have been mixing their tree stand hunting with their deer calling. One hunter who wrote me from Indiana reported that he had been hunting deer for twenty-five years and over that span had experienced no problem at all taking whitetails

Many whitetail hunters like the advantages that tree stands offer.
Jim Hamilton photo.

with a bow. He said he had deer at thirty-five yards that wouldn't come any closer and paid no attention to the call.

In a letter-writing situation, it's hard to know all the details of a particular hunt. It struck me, however, that the deer was already at thirty-five yards. I, too, have noticed that sometimes deer aren't responsive when they're that close. Sometimes they are. Sometimes they're not. Perhaps thirty-five yards was as close as that deer was going to come.

But it got me to thinking about tree stand hunters and their use of the call. It also made me ponder my own calling and things that worked and things that didn't.

For one thing, experience has told me that all members of the deer family are extremely adept at pinpointing the source of a sound. If they hear it only once, it might fool them for a second. But by the second time they hear it, they can key in on that location from some distance away.

In terms of that piece of the puzzle and how it applies to tree stand hunters, it made me think that perhaps a straight-on call might cause some harm in certain circumstances. If the deer has a good chance to listen to a fairly loud noise, he just might be able to tell that this deer sound is coming from somewhere other than a creature at ground level. And while tree stand hunters readily climb trees, real deer don't.

That piece of deduction led me back to my elk hunting experiences and the calling I've done there. It's common practice among elk hunters, especially those who attach long grunt tubes to their calls, that they'll direct the noise of the call behind them. They'll point the tubes that way and try to throw the sound, hopefully making it a bit more difficult for the elk to pinpoint them.

I've tried the same thing with my deer calling and can report some success with it. By putting my hand over the end of my Deer Talk call, I can muffle the noise and direct it. By making the call softer, it's more difficult to detect its source. By directing it, hopefully I can get enough bounce off trees, rocks and anything else in the area that the sound becomes more diffused.

That's just my theory on it, anyway. I know that many tree stand hunters who simply blow the call have had luck bringing whitetails within range with it. And getting them within range is all a matter of degree anyway. That thirty-five-yard shot that the Indiana hunter had would be close enough for many bowhunters and would be a virtual gimme for a rifle hunter. And perhaps calling them any closer to a tree stand would be an open invitation to spook them out of the country. As I said, I just don't know.

I do know that the best hunters are the ones who tailor their hunting to the country which they plan to hunt. In some places, that means tree stands. In others, it's working deer from the ground. The best hunters are the ones who can choose the right method for the right terrain.

While hunters on the ground don't face the same kind of problem of having the deer pinpoint a sound in the sky, I can tell you that muffling the call and trying to direct its sound elsewhere works well here, too. The key for the ground hunter is to keep himself low so he or she looks more like an undefinable lump on the forest floor instead of a human being. When possible, go to your knees to call. Sit with your back against a tree to break up your outline. If necessary, go to a prone position and make your calls from there.

In either case—far above the ground or clinging to it closely—use the call as a teaser to get the deer to come closer whenever he stops. Blow the call softly, so the deer can barely hear it. Blow the call sparingly, so the mystery stays alive. If you blow the call too loud, you're giving yourself away and may spook the deer. If you blow it too often, it tends to lull the deer into a sense of security. They know another deer is over there. They don't know why it's calling so much. There's no reason to go over and see why it's calling so much.

Another thing to remember is that while a call may be effective, it's not a miracle-worker. All deer are individuals. Whitetails seem especially so. Each will react to a call just a bit differently. And there are some times when deer calling isn't always effective. You won't always call in every deer within earshot.

One thing I've noticed, for example, is that it's difficult to call in deer when they're intent on feeding. After a day in their beds and with an empty stomach, it's tough to pull them away from the feed bag in the evening. They'd rather be eating than responding to a call.

Even on the ground, you can lure in interesting deer like this albino mule deer.
Chris Fisk and Jason Schilling photo.

My best results have come in the morning, the late morning and at mid-day. At that time of day, their attention can be focused on the sounds a call makes and not the growling in their stomach.

No matter what you're trying to call, whether it's a deer an elk, a turkey or a goose, it's also easier to get the animals to move in a direction they already want to go. It isn't easy for instance, to get an animal to cross a river or stream just because you're calling on the other side. You won't necessarily be able to pull them across an opening if they want to stay in dense cover. They probably won't come across a canyon, a deep ravine, or an interstate highway. These are barriers to deer that they shouldn't be expected to surmount.

I've also learned to be patient. A deer that looks like he's stopped or suddenly begins to wander might just be sizing up the situation before he comes in any further. The whitetail may actually be starting to circle so he can get downwind from you. He might be unwilling to give up a secure area so quickly for a place that he doesn't feel is quite as secure.

As I said, what you're trying to create is something of a mystery for the deer. You want the whitetail to come over and investigate the little noises that it hears. Blow the call softly. Make the calls short. Be patient and let the whitetail wander in.

And, by all means, if you get into a situation where something isn't working, don't be afraid to experiment and try something new. Every hunter learns from his mistakes. Every hunter makes his or her own breakthroughs by experimenting. Every experiment stands a chance of making you a better hunter. Whether you're up in the air or planted firmly on the ground, deer calling is still the new frontier where the rules are only just being written now for a future of better hunting ahead.

The Great Ghosts

The biggest whitetail bucks you almost never see. They're like ghosts that drift in and out of hunters' lives.

That, perhaps, is one of the great mysteries of the species. How, for example, can a farm country whitetail grow so large when it's living so close to people? How can a whitetail of the North survive the rut and so many winters with

Gordon Eastman and I took a trophy whitetail buck from Montana.
Don Laubach photo.

deep snow and bitter cold? How can a whitetail anywhere sneak past so many hunters who are looking to hang their tag on him?

The answer to all of those questions is that big whitetails have simply learned to adapt. They've become accustomed to the many dangers they face and have developed survival skills so that they can overcome them.

For one thing, the biggest bucks seem to be the most nocturnal. You won't often catch them out in the open during daylight hours. You won't catch them very far from escape cover either. And once they've found secure cover, you'll have a hard time blasting them out of it.

In short, big whitetail bucks seem to learn and learn quickly. If they don't learn, they simply don't stay alive long enough to grow big.

The examples of their skills at coping with mankind are endless. Deer drives, for instance, rarely end up pushing the big bucks toward the hunters waiting at the end. The big bucks either hold in cover until the drivers are past, or they may find a way to sneak back through the line of drivers. Or they have escape routes that allow them to sneak out the sides of the drive. Or, if they do filter back through the line, they escape behind the drivers.

A Montana friend, Jay Archer, once had a front-row seat to watch a deer drive working down a creek bottom. He was hunting pheasants that day and took a break on a hill overlooking the creek bottom. Drivers were pushing their way through thick willows. Standers were waiting for the deer to come. And, he said, the bottoms were loaded with deer.

Few of those deer, however, ever came past the guys on stand. He said it was amazing. The thick cover ahead of the drivers was alive with activity. There were deer moving everywhere. But inevitably, the whitetails found places to circle around the end of the drive line or they found the cracks and creases in that line to filter back through it. The hunters on stand saw a few of the deer, but none of the big bucks. The lesson it showed him was how ineffective a drive could be in moving the big whitetail bucks.

To make a big drive effective, you have to have plenty of drivers and plenty of hunters on stand. Make sure your drivers are walking very close to one another. Make sure, too, that they have the area covered from one side to the other. If you allow deer a place to run around the ends of the drive line, they'll find it. Then, have enough people on stand that they can cover the end point of the drive and any places on the edge where deer might escape before they reach the end point.

If you don't have a great number of drivers, then you're better off with just two or three hunters. Put one of the hunters on stand, either in a tree or in a good ground location where deer are likely to move through. Have the other one or two hunters move through the cover in more of a random fashion around the person on stand. Have the hunters on the move do their work quietly. Then rely on the fact that those hunters are going to be bumping deer and having those deer move to elude them. In this more informal drive situation, there is no real beginning point and end point. The effectiveness of this drive is simply in getting deer up out of their beds and making them move, then hoping the deer happen to walk past the person on stand.

That may not sound nearly as effective, but believe me, it can work. Hunting with Curt Collins on the Yellowstone River bottoms of eastern Montana, I ended up taking a good whitetail buck that way. I was the hunter on stand. What I chose was a ground blind where I could watch a stretch of dry river channel that was about twenty feet wide and 200 yards long. On one side, there was the broad river bottom with rosebushes, Russian olive and tall cottonwoods for cover. On the other was a sizable point with thick willows and other good cover for deer.

While I waited on stand, Curt walked through the cover on the point. It was early in the day. There was no wind. And Curt told me later he could hear the deer moving all around him, not necessarily running, but just getting out of his way. He never saw a one. But they were obviously there. From time to time, I'd hear deer, too, and occasionally, one would cross that dry channel to escape to the other side. Whenever I saw one, I'd bring up the gun and check the deer out. When a doe crossed, I'd stay in the ready position in case a buck was following her. Eventually, my vigilance paid off when I checked out four does that crossed, one at a time. With my gun still at the ready, a decent five-by-five buck finally stepped out trailing the does. With a single shot, he was mine.

The same strategy would work for a lone hunter who happened to be in an area where other hunters would stir up the deer toward him. The key in either situation is that the person moving around is rarely going to see the deer. It's the person who's on stand that is going to get the action. Another key is that the random movements of the person walking is going to stir up the deer. That person isn't going to even try to push the deer in a particular direction. As I said before, you might be able to move the does, fawns and young bucks. But big bucks will usually go where they want, not where you want.

If there aren't any other hunters to move the deer around, an often effective strategy is using classic still hunting techniques. Still hunting is a term that describes walking an area very slowly and stopping often for long periods of time.

The first thing you've got to do is put yourself in an area where you know the big bucks will be hiding. Then plan to spend a long time in that area. Walk a few steps, then stop and keep your eyes and ears wide open. Usually, if the bucks are big, your best success will come in spotting deer right in their beds. To do that, the best way is to use binoculars to scan the cover, even if that cover isn't very far away. The binoculars will force you to focus on a particular spot and make it easier to spot the patch of fur, the antler tine, the blink of an eye or the twitch of an ear that will give away the presence of a deer.

I've had hunters tell me that big bucks will often hold tight even when a hunter is just a dozen feet away from them. They've seen bucks crawl on their knees under impenetrable tangles of tight brush. And they've had those bucks explode out of close cover after holding there for many minutes while a hunter stood nearby.

Spotting a bedded deer in tight cover isn't easy. In fact, it's one of the most challenging ways to hunt big bucks. It requires patience. It requires constant vigilance. But nobody said bagging a big buck was going to be easy, either.

In the weeks surrounding the rut, bagging a big whitetail buck becomes a bit easier because they're at least as interested in does as they are in their own survival. And while whitetail bucks always show some interest in a deer call, they seem especially vulnerable to it during that time period.

The biggest whitetail buck I've ever shot—and one of the biggest ever taken with a black powder gun in Wyoming— came during that span. And while you always think of big bucks only in terms of tight cover, I was able to call this buck right out into an open field.

The procedure was a classic example of the way I like to call and made a beautiful piece of videotape for Gordon

Eastman who was filming the whole thing. I was right out in the open, staying low to the ground. I used common doe sounds to interest him. I kept him in sight, blowing the call whenever he'd stop. Eventually, I worked that big five-by-five within forty yards of me before he caught my wind and spooked. That buck was running out of there as fast as he could when I hit the half-distress sound. The buck heard it at 100 yards and came to a full stop, standing broadside. When he stopped, I was ready and fired a .54 caliber bullet that spelled the end for the trophy buck.

The buck was a good one, perhaps the best I'll ever take. It's not that I won't be looking for a better one in the years to come. It's just that I may not find him. As I said before, big whitetail bucks are like ghosts that drift into and out of a hunter's life.

In fact, in looking back to last season and the fine Wyoming whitetail, the thing that pleases me the most about the hunt was that the Deer Talk call gave me a second chance with that buck. It's true, I'd called the buck to within forty yards, but at that point, I didn't really have a shot. When the buck bolted, all I would have had was a single shot at a hard-charging deer that would hardly have been called a great opportunity. When that half-distress sound stopped that deer, it gave me a second chance, a good shot at a standing deer at 100 yards that I wouldn't have had in the years before the call came along.

How much was that second chance at a big buck worth to a whitetail hunter? Believe me, when you're talking about a shot at one of the great ghosts of the whitetail world, it made that deer call worth its weight in gold.

BASIC HUNTING STRATEGIES

Basic Equipment

For the most part, my wife is a very understanding person. Over the years, she has allowed me to hunt and fish with few time restrictions. She has politely nodded her head and smiled when I prattled on about some hunting experience that meant a lot to me and probably very little to her. She has tolerated deer carcasses hung in the garage for aging. She has arrived at fashionable affairs in four-wheel drives. She has even put up with my hunting buddies.

But even an understanding person like my wife has her limits. One of them I learned early in the marriage. That was the time when I scheduled a deer and elk hunting trip which kept me out of town on our wedding anniversary. I did it just one time. It didn't matter that I arranged for flowers to be delivered before I left. It didn't matter either that I drove thirty-some miles out of the mountains to reach a pay phone so I could call her that day. My absence that one year long ago still nettled her. I have been reminded of that absence every year since—and I've had a lot of years to be reminded.

The other thing that my most understanding wife has a hard time understanding is what I call basic deer hunting equipment. Each year, I'll describe to her something I'm planning to buy and she'll ask me why.

"It's just basic equipment," I'll respond.

"I thought you bought your basic equipment last year and the year before that," she'll say.

"Well, I did. But this is some more basic equipment."

"More basic equipment? Just how much basic equipment is there?"

"That's a tough one to answer. You see, there's basic equipment and there's more basic equipment and there's upgraded basic equipment," I'll say.

Then she'll just shake her head, walk away and remind me one more time that I'd better not be gone for our anniversary again like I always am.

End of discussion.

What I said was really true though. Basic equipment is something that a hunter puts together each year and improves on throughout his lifetime. It's really a never-ending process that changes with time and technology.

Take your standard deer gun, for example. That topic alone has fueled more friendly hunting feuds than almost anything else. What's best? Who really knows?

I can tell you that the hottest cartridge in the woods used to be a .30-30 Winchester. More deer have probably been killed by that one caliber than any other and perhaps all others. And though it continues to be a hot number for a lot of hunters, there are those who will tell you that its days of supremacy are long gone.

The same could be said for the venerable .270 Winchester as the powerful, flat-shooting, long-reaching round, though that, too, will start more than its share of arguments. The long-distance hunters of the West will point to the 7 mm.

Remington magnum as the new long-reaching round on the block. Against the 7 mm., the .270 just doesn't cut it—or so they say.

The truth of the matter is that there are a wide range of calibers that will do the job for the rifle-toting deer hunter of today. In tight situations that don't demand long-distance shots, the .30-30 is still a good weapon. The .270 has always been a good deer round, too. And so will a lot of others like the .243 Winchester, 6 mm. Remington, .250 Savage, .257 Roberts, .280 Remington, .308 Winchester, or .30-06 Springfield, to mention a few.

As a rule of thumb, I wouldn't recommend a rifle that shoots a bullet of less than 100 grains in weight. But I know able marksmen are shooting at and taking deer each year with calibers that throw bullets lighter than that. As to a caliber that's too heavy, I don't know of one. After all, shotgun slugs can weigh an ounce and that's a lot of lead.

The key, instead, for deer hunters is to make sure the gun they plan to use is accurate and that they can handle it well. The 7 mm. Remington magnum, for example, is one of the calibers that has a reputation for punishing a shooter with heavy recoil. If you can't handle the recoil without developing a flinch—and there's no lack of honor to admitting you don't like the physical pounding of a load like that— don't shoot a 7 mm. magnum.

If you plan to use a shotgun with slugs, make sure it has sights both front and rear or don't plan to shoot it at deer beyond the range of ten or twenty yards. With good adjustable sights, a slug gun can be very accurate and deadly to seventy-five or more yards.

The important things are to know the gun you're using, to make sure it's matched to the type of hunting you're doing and to be well-practiced at the ranges you plan to shoot. Western hunters will probably need a far-reaching gun with good telescopic sights of at least four-power and perhaps a three-by-nine variable. Eastern deer hunters, who usually don't have to cope with long-range shooting, can often get by just as nicely with a rifle with a heavier bullet that may not shoot so flat. They can often do just as well with open

Hunters should tailor their efforts to the equipment they have.
Mark Henckel photo.

sights or, perhaps, a low power telescopic sight. Once you've got the gun and sights in place, practice during the summer months at the ranges you expect to shoot at when deer season arrives.

Changes in rifle technology may mean that your basic gun equipment changes from time to time. At least, that's the excuse I've always used on my wife when I wanted a new gun. Sometimes she bought it. Sometimes she didn't.

Just as guns have changed, so have other pieces of basic equipment. Take clothing, for example. When I started hunting, if it was made of wool and patterned in red and black buffalo plaid, it had to be clothes for deer hunting. In just about every deer hunting state and province, that red color has gone the way of the blaze hunter orange. But that isn't the only change in deer hunting clothes.

Back in the days when everyone wore wool, noisy clothing wasn't a concern. Since the advent of nylon and synthetic blends, noisy clothing has been. It's only in recent years, it seems, that clothing manufacturers have been able to make synthetic fabrics as quiet as the old wools used to be. One of the newcomers on the block is fleece which has all of the quiet of wool, but had better be worn with something to cut the wind if you're to get much warmth out of it. Each company also seems to have their cotton-like fabric which they're touting as quiet in the woods. Perhaps most surprising of all, in this day of more and more synthetics, wool still remains the standard by which all other fabrics are measured when it comes to warm, durable and comfortable hunting clothes.

One of the most important pieces of equipment that a hunter has is his footwear. Here, too, you'll get plenty of arguments over what's best. Everyone has their favorite brand and style. To some extent, that is because of the varying conditions of weather and terrain that hunters face coast to coast. The soft forest floor of many parts of the East stands in stark contrast to the rocks and cactus found in the West. The heat of the South poses different problems than the snow and cold of the North.

If I had to pick one aspect of footwear, however, that seems to cut across all boundaries, it's the sole and how it contributes to the hunter's ability to move quietly. For me, the best answer has always been the air bob sole. It's made of rubber, which provides good traction even in severe cold when many of the plastic soles get hard and slippery. It has a good grip for rocks and soft soil alike. And it's a quiet sole that won't scuff on the hard surfaces and seems to move through the forest without breaking as many sticks that find their way beneath your feet as a hard sole might.

The ability to walk quietly can put you in position to sneak up on animals that will spook out ahead of you with boot soles that make more noise. The traction is important so you don't stumble, fall and hurt yourself. Believe me, deer hunters seem to spend most of their days in places that they really wouldn't want to crawl out of.

The key ingredients of the basic equipment you put on your body is to have it so that you can be comfortable in it all day long. That means a good hat, good coat, good pants, good socks and good boots. And, as I tell my wife often, that means upgrading the basic things I put on my body from time to time. It may also mean purchasing more than one set of clothes for hunting.

In the West, for example, we've learned that deer season here can mean almost anything in terms of temperature. We've had sun-baked 90-degree days clear into November. We've had 20-degree days and deep snow in September. The answer is to have two sets of hunting clothes for deer season. One is for warm weather wear. The other is quality cold-weather equipment. If you're only out hunting for the day, it isn't much of a problem in deciding what to take along. But if you're planning an extended hunting trip or a journey into the backcountry, you'd better plan on taking both sets along.

I can remember one year when I looked forward to a week-long September bowhunting trip into the backcountry. We packed into the mountains on horseback, looking forward to the gorgeous autumn weather and spectacular scenery we had in the previous year. Nights were in the 20s and daytime highs soared into the mid-60s and low-70s. We had golden aspens to hike through and cool green forests. It was crisp mornings and shirt-sleeve afternoons and the beauty of the mountains all around us. But that was the previous year. Instead, we faced a day-long snow on the first day and solid snowcover for the rest of the week. Nighttime temperatures hovered around the zero mark. Daytime highs were lucky to approach the 30 mark beneath leaden skies that kept spitting intermittent snow for the entire week. I slept in a stoveless tent and kept a good deal of my clothing on all night long. During the day, I stayed warm enough but I ended up wearing almost every stitch of clothing that I brought. And with the wet conditions that persisted throughout our stay, I had a hard time keeping my clothes dry enough to keep me warm. It was a good lesson on mountain weather during hunting season. And it's one that I've never forgotten in all the years since.

Mountain weather, in particular, seems to catch hunters unaware every year. Equinox snowstorms blow in and may stay for a couple of days or a week. It's something you have to be prepared to handle. But the same thing can be said for deer hunting anywhere. A chilling rain, unseasonable snow, or even heat-sapping cold wind can put the hunter into a life-or-death situation.

That need for preparation extends beyond your basic clothing. It also includes the things you take along with you. In my own case, I have a fanny pack that remains loaded throughout the year for whenever I need it.

The contents of the fanny pack are basic. It holds matches, a flashlight, extra batteries, toilet paper, first aid kit, knife, knife sharpener, compass, rope, candy bars and binoculars among other things. That fanny pack is strapped on whenever I head into the field, whether it's for a quick half-hour walk during scouting or an extended hunting trip.

What you put in a pack depends on your needs. I've talked to other hunters who have various ways to start a fire in their packs. I know one who has a signal flasher. I know others who have space blankets, garbage bags, extra hats or scarves, a spare camera, film and even fishing line and hooks in their packs.

The important thing to remember is to take the pack along whenever you head into the field. It can't help you if it's left behind. And even a short trip can turn into an ordeal of injury, illness or getting yourself lost where your fanny pack might end up saving your fanny.

In the future, it's my bet that a good deer call will also become an indispensable piece of equipment. Just as the duck hunters and turkey hunters wouldn't think of heading out without a call, the deer hunters, too, will pack them along. It's just another piece of basic equipment that will be added to the list of necessities.

The guns, the clothes, the boots, the fanny pack—put it all together and you don't really have many fancy frills. They're all basic hunting equipment. They're all things you'll need to gather and improve on as your hunting career unfolds.

To a wife, that might sound like an endless list of buying things just to have them. After all, if you survived last season without some things, you probably can survive this one, too. Who needs the extra details? In your defense, as you try to justify the new purchases to yourself and others, I can tell you that successful hunting is built on paying attention to details.

Hunters in the past wouldn't have thought of heading into the hills without their best gun and their favorite pair of woolens. Hunters of today take their best guns, too, along with their best hunting clothes—wool or otherwise—their fanny packs and, of course, their deer calls.

Tracking Before and After

Spoor. Spoor? What the heck is a spoor? I can remember asking myself that very question often in my early hunting life. Everybody was doing something with spoor. They'd be looking for it. They'd be happy they found it. But what the heck was it that they found?

My first introduction to spoor was doubtless in one of those heavy-duty African hunting pieces that used to grace the pages of *Field and Stream* or *Outdoor Life* magazines. Sir Lord Oddbottom or some other English guy was probably hunting lions. The exotic setting would put me in the mood. The excitement of the hunt would build. Then, BAM!, I'd be smacked with that word again. Spoor. I didn't know what the heck it was. But it sure seemed important to those African guys.

When I got old enough to branch beyond the pages of those outdoor magazines and begin ruffling through the pages of a *Webster's Dictionary*, I finally found out what spoor really was. According to my own desktop *Webster's* today, spoor is defined as "the track or trail of an animal, especially of a wild animal hunted as game."

Why the heck didn't they say so. Tracks. Trails. The prints and paths that wildlife leaves behind when it moves through an area. I grew up with all those things. But we sure didn't call them spoor. And nobody else in our parts called it that either.

Winter whitetail deer yards can produce a maze of tracks.
Frank R. Martin photo.

Basic Hunting Strategies

While the language may be different and the location of our hunting is oceans apart, the importance of being able to read the sign that animals leave behind is just the same whether you're hunting the wilds of Africa or the wilds of North America. The tracks and trails that animals leave behind are like the daily newspaper and the history book of the creatures that live there. You need to know how to read them before you take a shot and you especially need to know how to read them after you shoot.

The ability to read tracks and trails is an acquired one. Each time you spend time studying them, you add to your knowledge. To become really good at it, you spend lots and lots of time studying them.

The easiest time to read and study tracks is when there's snow on the ground. If you're hunting, you cross a set of tracks and simply decide to follow them. Tracking, however, is more than just following tracks to their source. It's also deciphering the things the animal is doing along the way.

Some tracks are simple to decipher. A deer that wanders back and forth is usually feeding. If the animal heads out in a straight line and never wanders, it's on the move from one spot to another. These tracks are typical of migrations from the high country to lower ground. Tracks that go up a mountain slope are usually headed for bedding areas. Tracks that go down are usually headed toward feeding areas.

In my own jaunts in the forest or out in the fields, I try to notice all the tracks I see. The reason is simple. Over the years, I've noticed that areas with a lot of squirrel, rabbit or bird tracks also tend to hold bigger game like deer and elk. Areas devoid of small game are usually devoid of big game, too.

One good way to hone your tracking skills is to head out in the summer when there isn't any snow on the ground. There are several advantages to this. For one thing, summer game tends to be more at ease than game during the winter. Food is more available. Deer tend to travel less. If you only can unravel the tracks and trails, you're likely to see the deer that made the tracks.

Another plus for the summer tracker is the fact that if you can follow an animal on bare ground, any other kind of tracking is a snap. To follow a deer without snow, you've got to look for tracks in the dust, the sand or the mud. In fields of tall grass, look for the line of bent stems that indicate an animal went that way. In forests deep with fallen leaves, look for the leaves that have been disturbed, the ones stepped down and the ones kicked up.

If you lose a summer trail, that's when you really get to put your deer knowledge to work. You go to where you last found the animal's trail and try to second-guess the animal. You imagine that if you were a deer, where would you head next. Then you go there and try to cut his trail again.

That may sound like a difficult task to learn and one that a novice hunter might never master, but you'd be amazed at how good you can get at second-guessing. It's at times like these that all your previous tracking experience comes into play and you end up acting on hunches and tendencies of deer tracks you've followed before. In that way, it almost becomes a sixth sense, something you rely on without really knowing why.

I found myself in just such a situation on an elk hunt once during the Montana archery season. Bowhunting tends to put more demands on a hunter than rifle hunting simply because the animal rarely drops in its tracks when you hit them. Rather than knocking them over with the force of the gunshot, a killing shot with a bow relies on the animal dying through blood loss.

On this hunt, I had used a Cow Talk call to lure a four-by-five bull within thirty-five yards. After the arrow hit the bull, he whirled and began running off through the timber at top speed. Immediately, I got back on the call, since that can often stop them, but I could hear the bull crashing through branches as he raced off in the distance.

I knew I hit the bull, so I waited for a half-hour before even looking for my arrow. There was no snow to help and the place the bull stood when I hit him was barely visible. I

Basic Hunting Strategies ■

couldn't find the arrow. I couldn't find a drop of blood. All I knew was the general direction in which he ran.

I swept back and forth in that general direction, looking for a spot of blood, a wisp of hair, the tell-tale tracks. I found nothing for more than 200 yards. All I was doing was letting the sound of the bull's departure and the lay of the land guide me in my search. Finally, I stood at what seemed like a crossroads. To my right was a mountain slope dotted with ponderosa pines, juniper and scattered brush. To my left was an open park marked with just a few small clumps of pines.

What to do? Which way did the bull go? I stood there for quite a while, wondering which way to turn. Finally, for reasons I don't fully know, I opted for the clearing to my left. It just seemed like the right way to go. And I didn't go twenty-five yards into that clearing when I turned to my left and saw the bull, stone dead and piled up in a small clump of pines. The fletchings sticking from the bull's side answered the final question as to why I never found the arrow.

Looking back, I'm sure that all the tracking I'd done in the years leading up to that hunt helped me greatly. I followed a general direction without any sign to help me and ended up walking straight to the downed animal. Luck certainly helped me along, too. Without any luck, I'd probably still be combing that mountain slope in search of the elk. On the other hand, you can't totally discount the hundreds of miles of trails that had been put behind me. You couldn't dismiss the thousands of tracks that I'd seen and studied. Every piece of the puzzle helps in putting together the big picture.

As I said before, if you plan to bowhunt for deer, your tracking skills have to be especially sharp. Following a blood trail is the difference between a successful hunt and a nightmare.

There are some standard rules of thumb that have been passed on over the years in regard to blood-trailing. Among them are:

- Waiting at least a half-hour before following the trail;
- Marking the drops of blood with bits of toilet paper or marking tape so you can go back and retrace your steps if you lose the trail;
- Following up a hit quickly if rain or snow threatens to wipe out the trail;
- Using a bright lantern or powerful flashlight to spot the drops of blood at night which tend to glisten in the light;
- Finding a partner to help you because two sets of eyes are invariably better than one;
- Not forgetting to look above the ground as well as on it for blood because it can be smeared on leaves, grass, twigs or the bark of trees;
- Remembering that animals that are hit often head downhill and may head toward water.
- Going slowly and scanning the area ahead of you carefully to spot the downed animal. And being prepared to make another shot if you need to finish it off.

In the past, many of those lessons were passed from one generation of bowhunter to the next. Others were learned the hard way, in the field after you actually hit a deer.

All that has changed for the better in recent years, however. Now, the National Bowhunter Education Foundation has put together a Bowhunter Education course that will speed your learning process.

Having sat in on one of the courses with my son, I can tell you they're excellent and not just for bowhunters. Any hunter can benefit from the lessons learned in the course.

The National Bowhunter Education Foundation also has put together a little booklet called the "Big Game Recovery Guide," written and illustrated by Wayne Trimm that would be a welcome addition to anyone's hunting pack. It offers advice and guidelines on trailing and recovering game that has been hit. The booklet is a quick and easy read and offers fine advice. The address of the Foundation, as listed on the back of the booklet, is Route 6, Box 199, Murray, KY 42071.

Basic Hunting Strategies ■

The only major addition I'd like to make to the trailing and recovery effort is to expand on the need to do so quietly and to add the deer call to your efforts. I've been in on deer trailing expeditions alone and with other hunters. I've done it quietly. And I've done it with a lot of talking and communication.

If the trackers are talking and the deer isn't dead when they approach it, the animal invariably jumps up and runs off. If you approach the animal quietly, there is less chance of that, but it still happens.

In my future trailing of a wounded deer, I'm planning on using the deer call for the same reasons I blew on that elk call as soon as the wounded bull I told you about started to run. Just as the elk call calms an elk, the deer call tends to have a calming effect on deer. Just as the elk call seems to make elk curious, the deer call works the same. So as I work slowly along the blood trail of the deer, I'm going to blow on the deer call from time to time. For one thing, it will mask my own sounds and could make the wounded deer think that I'm just another deer on his trail. For another, it might hold him there instead of making him jump.

I'm banking on the fact that the addition of the deer call to my blood trailing repertoire will make it easier to get up on animals that may be mortally hit, but haven't died yet. It's something I plan to experiment with in the future. And I'm dead certain that it will work. If there's one word of warning in doing it that way, however, it will be to make positive identifications of the deer that I see. With the pulling power of the deer call, it's just as likely another deer will wander in as will the one that I hit. And if I shoot at the wrong deer, the last thing I'll want is to have more deer hit than I have tags for.

Learning as much as you can about tracks and trailing before you head into the field during deer season will help make you a better hunter. Once you get into the field, the lessons you have learned will come back to you. Add in the experiences you have with deer on the hunt and you'll get a more complete picture of the basic skills you need to find success as a deer hunter. You'll be better able to find the animals you shoot. And you'll enjoy much more the simple pleasure of reading the signs that wildlife leaves behind.

Deer Patterns

All animals are creatures of habit—even you are. On most days, you get up from bed at about the same time. You have about the same number of meals at the same times each day. You go to the same bed at about the same time and sleep for about the same number of hours. It's a pattern that's developed over the course of your lifetime and it's something you've grown to be comfortable with.

Deer are very much the same. If you witness a deer feeding at a certain spot at a certain time one day, it's very likely you'll find them doing the same thing the next. If you locate a deer bedding in one area, it's likely you'll find him in the same general area on succeeding days.

Patterns—we all have them, deer and man alike. And once we're in a pattern, we tend to hold to it for quite some time. Yet it's in recognizing those patterns that deer use and making the most of them that hunters become successful. That's not to say deer will stay in patterns forever. Changes in the season, changes in the weather, changes in human activity around them will all trigger changes in the deer. But here, too, if you recognize the changes in the patterns you'll be successful.

That may seem like a contradiction of sorts—deer doing the same thing is a pattern and deer changing is a pattern. But it's really not.

Let me explain it with an example. There's a whitetail spot that I frequent which has a well-established morning pattern. There's a clearing to the west where the animals will feed during the night. There's a bedding area to the east where the whitetails will hole up during the day. In between there is a place I like to sit and wait for the whitetails to move through. That's fairly simple.

Success at the spot, however, depends on a number of fac-

Whitetails will often gather in specific areas during winter.
Mark Henckel photo.

tors. Every year, the whitetails use the pattern—that's a given. But the number of deer changes from year to year— that's one variable. Some years there is a good buck worth filling your tag, some years there isn't one worth shooting— that's another variable. But the biggest variable of all is pressure from other hunters.

From years of hunting the spot, I know that the time when the deer will move past my stand will depend on pressure from other hunters. In most years and on most days, the movement of the deer out of their feeding area and toward the bedding area will be triggered by the first sounds of other hunters' vehicles arriving at about dawn or the first sounds of other hunters walking to their stands. For that reason, I know I've got to get to my stand well before first light. If I can sneak in while it's still dark and sit quietly well ahead of the other hunters' arrival, I should have deer moving past me just at shooting time and in the first half-hour of legal hunting. If I get there late, I might as well head to somewhere else. That's one solid pattern.

Inevitably, however, you'll hit one of those rare days during Montana's five-week deer season when the other hunters don't arrive. Maybe it's because it's unseasonably cold. Perhaps it's because of wet weather. Possibly, it's just one of those strange days when no one decides to hunt. Whatever the reason, there's no one there to bump the deer out of their feeding area and send them my way at dawn. The deer are left to depart their feeding area at their own whim. On those days, I've had deer filter past me until 10 in the morning. With no outside factor to push them, they change their formerly solid pattern. That might mess up another hunter newer to the area. But I've been hunting the spot long enough that I recognize this as a pattern, too.

As you can see, some patterns are easy to pick up quickly. Others take much more time. You can tell right away which fields the deer are using for feeding. With a little more time, you can unravel the mysteries of the deer's bedding area and even the preferred routes that lead between the two. But the patterns that are dictated by special conditions, such as the disturbance by other hunters, will very likely take much longer to detect.

Every consistently successful hunter knows about patterns whether they consciously tell you about them or not. Some hunters will be able to describe the animals' patterns in great detail. Others simply know that they'll find deer at a particular place at a particular time of year. They've picked up on a pattern almost in spite of all the other details in a deer's life.

Many hunters think patterning is only possible with whitetails. They've said that mule deer live a much more wide open lifestyle in the open West. That might be true to some extent. It is true that whitetails live a much tighter lifestyle, especially in areas where they can survive year-round without major migrations. In those places, you can spot them more easily and tie them more closely to specific feeding areas and bedding areas within a much smaller piece of real estate. But don't fool yourself. Mule deer follow patterns too, even if they do it on a much grander scale.

The best example of this is the mid-migration patterns of

The older mule deer does will be the leaders of groups of deer.
Bob Zellar photo.

mountain mule deer bucks. Most people know that the best places to find those bucks in the summer and early in fall is in the high country. They often hold above or right at timberline. They'll inhabit the high basins. They'll exist amid the shale rock, the high flowers and the steep slopes. And, in these places, they'll find a measure of solitude during the summer months, letting the winds of the high country keep the flies at bay while the people stay in the valleys far below.

But there's a change that takes place about the time the hunting season arrives. It isn't necessarily triggered by deep, early snows. It's just a certain time of year that arrives when the big bucks seem to pull out of the high country. They'll move to intermediate areas, somewhere between their summer range and winter range. Then they'll stay there until the pressures of winter and the rut finally drive them to the low country.

It's the type of situation I've run into often over the course of a lifetime of hunting. Yet it's still a little difficult to pin down as to exactly where they'll go, when they'll go there and why they pick this middle area as the best place to be.

The key is to find these areas and that's not always easy. We had one drainage I hunted, for example, where there was an easily-recognizable gene pool of deer. The bucks were big. They had a lot of points. They had a lot of abnormal points. You'd find them at the head of this creek drainage every summer. After the hunting season, you'd find these bucks on the winter range below. But during the hunting season, they'd seem to just disappear.

It took some years to find where these bucks were going. But, finally, I located them. There was an intermediate area that'd move into clear over in another creek drainage. Rather than following the up-the-mountain-in-spring and down-the-mountain-in-fall migration patterns that most people envision, these bucks would travel across the face of the mountain into a different drainage entirely.

The place they pulled into was typical of the other intermediate areas where I've found big bucks. These bucks had migrated into an area that had a lot of cliffs and a lot of rocks. It was tight and steep, yet it held all the ingredients of life for the deer. It had food. It had water. It had lots and lots of security because, frankly, the going for hunters would have been extremely tough. As a result, the area offered solitude for the deer because few hunters ever went there.

Basic Hunting Strategies

On another occasion, hunting partner Mark Wright and I stumbled into another one of these intermediate holding areas while we were out hunting for bighorn sheep. Once again, it was an area with a lot of rocky cliffs. The country was also broken enough that you could never see very far and couldn't effectively glass it with binoculars or spotting scopes. As a result, we just did our best to hike through the rocks and ended up jumping bucks in the area almost wherever we went.

The amazing thing about the area that Wright and I found was that the country in the drainage above it was not known for holding many deer during the summer. As a result, we knew these bucks were coming in there from some other drainage. They were pulling into the area laterally, not from above. And they likely were leaving it laterally also when they headed on toward the winter range.

Another amazing thing about this intermediate area and many of the others I've found is that they tend to hold big bucks. Oh, you might find a few small ones. But, for the most part, these are the hiding places that the truly big mule deer bucks use to wait out the hunting season.

If there are common denominators to these areas, it's that they tend to be remote. There are a lot of rocks. There are often a lot of cliffs. They usually have scattered timber. They tend to be on steep slopes. They may have small benches. And they're invariably somewhere in the middle in terms of elevation. They're not on the mountaintops. They're not in the valleys.

Once you locate one of these places, you'll find that they hold big bucks every year. The individual bucks may change with the passage of time. But the trait to move to these areas is passed along from one generation to the next. That means the future of these intermediate areas may be somewhat fragile. If you locate one of these spots, then gather up all your friends and go there and everyone fills their tag, you could conceivably wipe out the tradition. As long as you don't overharvest the area, however, you can go back and expect to find bucks there every year.

Big bucks will often hold in intermediate areas.
Don Laubach photo.

How do you go about locating one of these intermediate areas? I can tell you it isn't easy. They tend to be fairly small. They're also relatively remote and difficult to get to. All I can say is that they'll come with time and experience. The more you knock around the mountains and spend time in your hunting area, the more likely you are to find one. Also, you can speed the process by carefully studying topographic maps and making note of the areas that seem to have all the ingredients listed above.

Whether it's a complex pattern or an easy one, and whether it's a whitetail or a mule deer, learning about the patterns of deer is going to take an investment in time. You're going to have to spend days in the field both in and out of hunting season if you're going to do it right.

During the season, you'll have to use your powers of observation on the deer you see and the fresh tracks left behind. Before or after the season, you'll need to be able to read tracks and old sign to determine the places where bucks have rubbed their antlers, left droppings behind or

Basic Hunting Strategies ■

made a hard-beaten path. Over time, you'll put all these ingredients together and learn what your deer are doing, perhaps even throughout the year.

If you're pressed for time or you have to do your hunting within the time frame of a short season, become an expert on where deer will be and what they're likely to be doing during that narrow time span each year. If you have to concentrate on one week, for example, then key in on that and know what the effects of different weather conditions and hunting pressure will do to the deer during that specific time.

Believe it or not, that narrow time frame isn't as big a handicap as you might think. Even in Montana with its long seasons and abundant deer population, many hunters concentrate their efforts that way. Those who have patterned their deer population well know that they'll move into a particular area at about the same time each year. They know what snow conditions it might take to move them in there earlier or later. And they'll focus their hunting time on those deer under those conditions. They might not be experts at all deer under all conditions at all times, but they've got that one pattern nailed down tight and make the most of it every season.

It's that background knowledge—either broad or narrow—that's needed to put you in the right place at the right time to be in contact with the whitetails or mule deer you're after. Without that knowledge, you'll be relying totally on luck to stumble into deer. And, one way or the other, you've got to have the deer if you hope to be successful.

If you don't put yourself into the right place at the right time, no amount of deer calling expertise is going to pull a good buck within range. Without the deer, you can have the best clothing, the perfect gun and all the other skills necessary and it won't do you any good.

So the best advice I can give you is to invest the time and learn the patterns of the deer you plan to hunt. It will help make you a successful deer hunter year, after year, after year.

Putting It All Together

I had a friend once who was just getting started in deer hunting. He had the bug bad. Every time we got together, he began asking me questions about deer hunting. He'd talk of his own experiences in the woods. And he even let me prattle on with story after story after story without one word of complaint. As I said, the man had it bad.

Finally, he asked me, "Of all the things you've told me and the advice you've given me, what is the most important thing that makes you a good deer hunter?"

I suppose it shouldn't have, but the question stopped me cold. Most important? One thing? The more I thought about it, the more complicated the question became. What is most important? Experience—that's important. Being quiet in the woods—that's important. Being able to spot deer before they spot me—that's important. Good gun, good clothes, good hunting camp—that's important. Being a good caller—that's important, too. Now which one is the most important? I just couldn't pick.

The truth of the matter is that all these things are important parts of being a good deer hunter. One feeds off the other. Any weakness in any of these areas and they all fall down like an unbalanced house of cards.

"Let me think about that one and I'll get back to you," I finally told my friend. And, after much thought, I did get back to him with one word—details. Hunting success is built on dozens of them. Each one plays a part in the good things that can happen. Each one can play a part in the mishaps.

The consistently successful hunter is the one who most often puts it all together and can do so on a regular basis. That hunter is the master of many details. He has learned his lessons through books, conversations or, more likely, through hard experience over the years, learning from his own mistakes and those of others.

One of the first whitetail bucks I had a chance to draw a bead on taught me about one of the hard lessons about details. I can't exactly remember how old I was at the time.

I remember I was horribly young, horribly excited and horribly crushed by the whole experience.

I'd gone into the woods and found a perfect stand for opening morning. I studied the deer trails. I got into the stand well before first light. I shivered in the cold and waited. I had scoped out the whole area. I knew where the deer would be coming from and where they'd be going.

About ten minutes after legal shooting time arrived, my dreams were answered with a forkhorn whitetail just fifty yards away. It was a young buck—perfect for a young hunter—and he was pussy-footing along the trail, intent on the area ahead of him and unaware I was watching him. In the gray still of the early morning forest, I put a bead on that deer's chest and pulled the trigger. And the deer ran away.

How could I have missed? I went over to where the deer was standing and looked for blood. None. I looked for hair. None. I followed the running deer's tracks and still could find no sign that I hit him. So I walked back to where the deer was standing and looked all over again. It wasn't until I began walking back toward my stand that I saw the reason I missed that buck. A small sapling, barely an inch in diameter, had a neat half-circle cut into its trunk. About halfway to the deer, it had taken the bullet and adjusted its direction just enough so that it missed the buck entirely.

Ever since then, I've been especially careful to make sure my bullet has a clear path to its intended target. It's just a small detail—and, frankly, in that early morning light I might not have been able to detect the sapling—but the experience that day long ago made me painfully aware of how easily a bullet can be deflected and how a shot at a buck can be missed.

We talked earlier about the basic equipment necessary for hunting success. Those are more details. Patterning is another detail. And so is your ability with a deer call.

All of these things come together when you try to move quietly through an area that you know will hold deer. What you have to picture is that the deer are paying attention to details as well. They've had to be attuned to details from the day they were born to avoid predators like coyotes, bears and mountain lions or accidental death at the hands of man's cars, his farm machinery or the natural features of the land like ice-covered rivers or cliffs.

With the deer paying attention to details, you have to make sure that you don't make foreign noises while you're hunting them. The sound of a Velcro tab being ripped open on a pocket is a foreign noise to deer. The metallic sound of an arrow bouncing off an arrow rest is a foreign noise. The noise of a zipper on a day pack. The sound of a hard-nylon day pack rubbing against the brush. The sound of hunters talking. All of these sounds are small details when put in the context of a whole hunting trip, but all will alarm a deer, especially a big buck who has learned to associate those sounds with danger from man.

When you decide to use your deer call, you also have to pay attention to details and put together a good calling scheme. It isn't enough to know how to make the proper sounds.

To make a good calling setup, you have to envision where the deer are likely to appear. Do you have good visibility in that direction? Is the deer's approach clear of obstacles that might cause him to hang up such as creeks, fences, hills or heavy brush? You have to know the wind direction and wind speed. Too much wind and the sound of your calling won't carry very far. If it's from the wrong direction, the deer might catch your scent on the way in.

How about your calling position? What if the deer doesn't come in from the direction you predict? Will you be able to move to another spot easily and monitor the deer's approach? Or are you stuck in the brush so that you can't move easily? In good deer country, it's possible for deer to come in from almost any direction. You have to think about that before choosing your calling position.

Finally, how long should you stay in one spot and call? That's a tough detail, too. When there are two hunters not in synch, it's possible for one hunter to want to stay longer while the other is more impatient and seeks to abandon the

If you can lure in the lead doe, she'll bring the other deer with her.
Bob Zellar photo.

spot more quickly. At that point, it's a battle of wills and whoever is the strongest is going to impart his will on the other.

All of these things are details that can affect the success of your deer calling. All can make you or break you when you call in deer. And, honestly, there are few rules of thumb that truly apply to all situations.

I know that in my own experiences, both alone and with others, I've had to work out more than a few of these details. I've made my share of mistakes, too, and hopefully I learned from them.

In my earlier years with an elk call and deer call, I know I was much too impatient and perhaps too hasty in working many of these things out. I've called from bad positions and paid the price when animals came in and I couldn't get a shot. I paid the price, too, when I decided to abandon calling positions and stood up only to find that I spooked animals that were on their way in.

As a rule of thumb now, I usually stay in a calling spot for at least a half-hour. If I know there are animals around, I'll stay for at least a full hour. As to how much longer than that I might stay, that's all a matter of how secure I am in my position and my feelings that day.

Younger hunters might laugh at it, but in my years of hunting I've probably grown to appreciate the peace and serenity of deer country more than I did in earlier years. I always liked to call. But I've grown to like the country that I call in more and more. And I've grown to truly love the chance to be in that country with all the wildlife that lives there.

As a result, when I'm in a calling spot, making my calls and enjoying the outdoor world, I'm more likely to stay there and enjoy the experience rather than hustle off to another spot. If that sounds like old age or laziness on my part, rest assured that it has also produced more than its share of good results.

Often, I've had animals come in after long, long calling sequences at a particular spot. Why they come in more than an hour after I start calling, I don't know. Where they come from I really don't know. Maybe they're wandering in from a long ways off. Maybe they wander within range of the call. Maybe they're just testing my patience and making sure that the sounds are really genuine. All I know is that it takes some animals a long, long time to respond to a call. Because of that, one of the details I'm still perfecting in my hunting life is patience and I'm happy to say it's getting better all the time.

Most often now, I try to get into a more comfortable calling position that I can stay in for a long time. I make sure that I can see all around. I get into a position where I can shoot without any kinks. I get into a place where if I have to make a minor adjustment and move to a slightly different spot, I can do so without spooking the deer. All it takes is paying a little more attention to the details.

In regard to the variety of wildlife that I see, I should point out that both the Cow Talk elk call and Deer Talk deer call seem to work on far more than the species for which they were designed. Again, I don't really know why.

I know that, in my early work with elk calls, I noticed that birds like gray jays and pinyon jays seemed to flock around me when I called. I noticed that coyotes came in and drifted through the areas I was watching. I noticed the elk call seemed to interest mule deer and sometimes held them so I could take a shot.

Those observations have continued with my use of the deer call. This call also seems to interest a variety of animal species like coyotes and birds and even bobcats. In that regard, some varmint hunters have actually purchased my calls specifically for their coyote hunting and raved about their effectiveness.

The good thing about the calling is that it brings in a lot of animals that are exciting to see and, if you're hunting for coyotes, you might even want to take. But there's a downside to this that you should be aware of as well.

The calls also seem to be extremely effective on bears. If you're a black bear hunter, that's good. You can combine your deer and bear hunting and have a chance to fill either or both tags. But I've got to tell you that both the elk and deer calls have also worked on grizzly bears. That can be slightly unnerving if you're not hunting for them or aren't prepared to see one.

I heard of one hunter who was calling elk in a relatively tight timber situation with a Cow Talk call and looked around and had a grizzly stalking him. The bear was close enough that it gave the hunter more excitement than he really wanted. He knew about grizzlies. He knew he shouldn't run from a bear. But he couldn't convince his feet of that and he raced down the trail in hopes that the bear wasn't following him in the same direction. It turned out the bear had similar ideas of its own and raced in the opposite direction. No harm was done to either of them, but it provided one more detail that the elk caller would never forget. And it reinforced the notion that when you're calling deer, elk or any other species, that you've got to be able to see and know what's going on all around you.

All of these details are gained through experience—either

your own, mine or someone else's that you hear about. They're all the successful things and unsuccessful things that a hunter does. Putting them all together and paying attention to the details will determine how successful a deer hunter a person becomes. The choice is yours. You can ignore them all and hope to get lucky every year. Or, you can put together a strategy for consistent success that pays attention to details where all the luck you have is carefully crafted by you.

ADVANCED HUNTING STRATEGIES

Go Low and Slow

Sometimes, it's impossible to do anything wrong in your calling. You can call deer anywhere, from anywhere. That isn't normally the case. But it can work that way. Take the time I went down to the coffee shop at the gas station in the middle of Gardiner to share a cup with some friends.

First, you have to understand that Gardiner, where I live, is not a big town. Also, it's situated in great country for deer and elk. And in winter, when the deer and elk pour out of nearby Yellowstone National Park, it isn't uncommon to have these animals near town and sometimes in town. But that day I shared coffee with my friends is still unusual by any standards.

The day I'm talking about took place two winters ago. I had recently gone into production with my first Deer Talk calls. And my friends were asking me about how it worked.

"It's like magic," I told them. "You can call deer anywhere."
Needless to say, they were a bit skeptical.

Just then, I noticed some deer about seventy-five yards
away, on the other side of the fence, on the other side of the
highway. I figured I'd prove my point. Opening the door, I
called to the deer using my basic opening sequence of 555-
1212. I caught the deer's attention immediately. Before I
was even done with the sequence, the deer were moving
my way. Before they stopped, they had jumped the fence,
crossed the highway, and were right in the gas station, milling around the pumps.

That day, with those deer, you could have done anything.
They were exceedingly receptive. They hadn't been pres-
sured, like they might have been during hunting season. Everything turned out right. Needless to say, my friends were
impressed.

I've heard from other people that they've had similar luck
just calling out the windows of their cars. One salesman, in
fact, had to quit calling because the deer were threatening
to cross the lanes of a busy interstate highway and he didn't
want one to get hit.

While those kinds of stories are real attention-getters and
are guaranteed to raise some eyebrows, they only explore
one facet of deer calling and it's not the one that is likely
to be most productive for the deer hunter or the wildlife
photographer.

In all my calling, I've had the best luck when the deer
couldn't see me. It's like any calling, I guess. You might
catch the eye of an elk if you're standing in full view calling to him. He might even come partway toward you. But
he isn't likely to get very close to something he recognizes
as a man standing there. Wild turkeys are the same way.
They might gobble back at your calls. But if they see you,
they're going to keep their distance. The same holds true
of deer.

No matter what type of calling you do, if the animal can
see you, you're at a disadvantage. If they can hear you make
any sounds other than your calling, you're at a disadvan-

tage. If the animal can smell you, you're at a disadvantage.

What you want the deer to do is be looking for another deer.

To pull that off, it requires some careful consideration of where you're going to call from. You want to pick a spot where you can see the deer coming in, but where they have trouble seeing you. That may sound contradictory, but it really isn't.

For me, the key has always been body position. I've had my best luck, by far, calling from a low position. That might mean sneaking over a ridgetop on my hands and knees and then going to a sitting position with my back against a tree. It might mean simply dropping to my knees and staying low that way. Or, it might even be calling from a prone position.

By taking a low position, I've had deer come in to my calling and even come in close and not recognize me as a man. It's almost as if they're programmed to see man in just one way and that's standing upright.

When you add in the variable of the call, you're fooling their sense of hearing. They keep telling themselves that they hear a deer from your position. They almost refuse to believe that you're anything but a deer.

This notion of changing your own shape really isn't anything new. I can remember being on an elk hunt with Vince Yannone, of Clancy, Montana, a number of years ago when we pulled off just such a shape change on a whole herd of elk. The incident took place in the gloom of early morning while we were walking in toward an area where we planned to hunt. The problem was that there was a big herd of elk on an open hillside just 150 yards away from us that we didn't spot until we were out in the middle of an open field. It took that long for us to spot the elk. But every elk in the herd had seen us first.

"Bend over and grab my butt," Vince said.

"Do what and grab what?" I replied.

"Just do what I say. And bend over. We're going to make like a cow. I'm the head and you're the tail," he said.

Odd as it may sound, the scam worked. I bent over and followed Vince, who did his best to walk and move like a

You can get close to deer out in the open, if you just stay low.
Bob Zellar photo.

camouflaged Hereford might have. We cowed our way all
across that open field until we reached the security of the
timber beyond. The elk herd never moved. The elk just
watched us go.

How else could you explain it but that the change of shape
had somehow fooled the elk. It may have bewildered them,
but it allowed us to make our move. Had we been walking

upright, there's no doubt in my mind that the whole herd would have spooked.

In similar manner, I've had bowhunting friends tell me that they got themselves out of some tight spots by dropping to all fours and pretending that they were grazing as they moved out of sight of a watchful animal. That sounds pretty weird, too. But I'm sure it worked for the same reason. The animals were just not programmed to recognize a man in any position other than standing upright.

Going low and slow has even worked for me—often—in approaching animals or having them approach me in an open field. Once again, you have to stay low to the ground. And in open field situations, the lower the better, using the grass or the sagebrush or whatever is available to you. Another key to open field calling is to keep your movements to a bare minimum. Freeze when you can. If you have to move, make your movements slow and deliberate. As long as your movements are slow, that also seems to confuse the deer, which are used to more rapid movements from man.

It's only a theory, but I think the reason that deer—and mule deer especially—can be fooled out in the open is because they feel they can see any danger that might be there. If a man were standing upright, they'd spot him. If a coyote or wolf or bear was there, they'd see that. But the low form, that lump in the grass where the deer sounds are coming from? That seems to present no danger at all.

One of the things I've noticed about the deer that come in out in open field situations is that they seem to come in so unafraid. It's not like there's something lurking behind a tree or a bush that will leap out and get them. In the open situations, they just come in curious, wanting to know what's making the sound.

Their curiosity will sometimes bring them in amazingly close. I've had deer within ten or fifteen feet of me out in the open. I've had them looking at me. I've had them looking past me. I've had them totally confused.

One of the big advantages of the open field situation, and any calling station where you have a good view, is that you can tailor your calling to the reactions of the deer. As I've

Use your call only when deer stop to tease them to come closer.
Frank R. Martin photo.

said before, you don't really want to blow the call when the deer is on the move toward you. Hearing the call will only make the deer stop and listen. That only stalls the situation and is the exact opposite of what you want the deer to do. What you want to do is tease the deer, blowing the call only when it stops, to urge it to come closer.

Another aspect of the low and slow theory to remember is that you not only don't want the deer to see you as a man, you also don't want the deer to hear you. Any foreign noise is enough to put the deer off. That might mean a noisy zipper. It could be the brush of a hard plastic parka. It could be tearing open a Velcro tab on a pocket. It might be the metallic click of your binoculars touching your gun barrel. Or, it could be even the whispered talk between hunters.

Any of those things could be enough to put the deer off and ruin a calling situation. All of them are foreign noises that tell deer that there's something unnatural in the area.

In the end, that's a lot more frightening than an unidentified lump in the brush or in an open field that's making deer sounds.

Sometimes, of course, you don't need to be so careful. Sometimes you can make mistakes and get away with them. Sometimes you can have a situation that's so unnatural it's like mule deer milling around gas pumps. But it's the careless hunter and the wishful caller who would try to bank on times like those. Better to take caution instead and try to do it right. Stay low. Go slow. And good and productive deer calling will be your well-earned reward.

Scents and Sounds

When hunters wear camouflage, they're trying to fool a deer's eyes. When they call, it's fooling a deer's ears. Add in the use of scent and you've fooled the deer's nose, too.

While camouflage can be used in some states and in some seasons and is illegal in others, scents and sounds are almost universally legal during hunting seasons. The key here is to get past, or at least make a deer doubt, his defenses.

Talk to different hunters and I'm sure you'll get different answers as to which of the senses is most important for a deer. Some will say they rely most on those big ears and that hearing is their primary defense mechanism. Others will talk about their eyesight, especially among muleys and blacktails, and tell you that their ability to spot movement and danger is the way they protect themselves. But as for me, I've always been suspicious about that nose. Of all the senses that a deer has, their ability to smell has always mystified me and made me the most wary.

Think about it. One of the earliest lessons that a hunter learns is that you've got to have the wind on your side or the deer will smell you. Once the deer gets a whiff of man smell, that animal is gone. That's proven true for deer hunters since the first primitive man tried to move in on an animal from the upwind side.

When you watch deer that are uncertain about something,

you'll also notice that they always try to circle so that they can get to the downwind side. That's further evidence that they really rely on their nose when the going gets tough.

Last fall, while hunting whitetails, my feelings were only reaffirmed by an incident in South Dakota. One of my hunting partners had gotten a buck that we were forced to hang overnight in the field before we took it home. All we had to hang the deer from was a short tree. It took a little moving around and trying to get the deer situated so it would be safe. In the end, we muscled the deer up as well as we could so the coyotes wouldn't get it. We tied off the head and then raised up the back legs so that the deer was out of reach.

The first thing the following morning, we took the deer down and transported it. But chance had us hunting nearby the following day. Glassing back to the spot where we hung the deer, I noticed a whitetail doe was at the spot. For the next hour, I watched that deer as she smelled everyplace we had that deer. She even smelled the limbs of the short tree and nosed the spot where the buck's antlers had been.

It was three days after the deer was shot and almost two days since the buck had been hanging in that tree. But the doe was still able to detect the smells of that buck and, apparently, the smell was strong enough to hold her there for far more than a short period of time.

That's some sense of smell. Is it any wonder then that hunters have relied on a variety of methods to try and beat the scenting ability of deer. They work to keep their clothes scent free. They bathe and wash themselves with special soaps, including some incredibly icy dips in lakes and streams during the late hunting seasons. And they have learned to use a variety of coverup and attracting scents.

I've always wondered what deer thought when they smelled a mixture of perspiration and apple scent. I've wondered what kind of cigar-smoking skunk they must figure inhabits the woods. And I can only imagine the vision that a deer gets when you mix a pine tree and peanut butter sandwich. While I can only guess what a deer thinks, I know

Deer often rely more on their noses than their eyes to identify danger.
Michael H. Francis photo.

what wives think when the clothing comes home after hunters have doused themselves with these things.

My own feelings about scent have been biased by my elk hunting, of course. While hunters can't usually smell deer, they can smell elk. The tell-tale musk of elk is left behind in their beds and carried on the wind. You can literally tell when elk have been in the area simply by using your nose. As a result, I've always wanted my own sense of smell to be untainted when I was hunting. That's never the case when you douse yourself with coverup or attracting scents. All you can smell all day is pine or apple or dirt or urine.

My own twist on the scenting game has been to use an atomizer bottle to spray the air in situations when I knew I really needed a coverup. Invariably, I use doe-in-heat or cow-elk-in-heat urine scents. Then I'll mix a small amount of that urine with a greater amount of water in a ratio of about one part to ten. That way my own nose stays sharp and I can still confuse the nose of a deer.

Advanced Hunting Strategies

When I get a deer coming in downwind of me, I'll just spray the atomizer a few times and saturate the air with scent. Droplets will fall on the brush or grass or trees. The wind will carry the scent of those droplets downwind and my scent cover on that side will be complete.

I've used the system countless times on both deer and elk over the years. It works far more times than it doesn't. And I've had deer approach within feet of me on the downwind side without smelling me. My own theory for why it works so well is that I think saturating the air not only gives the deer a whiff of the scent, but must clog their sinuses to some extent. All I know is that when the deer and elk get a good dose of the saturated air, they'll often lick their noses repeatedly. Whether that's to make their ability to smell more acute or clear their sinuses, I don't really know. All I know is that it works.

Spraying situations generally come in two varieties. In one case, you've got the deer downwind already and they're coming in from a distance. In that case, you've got plenty of time to pull out your atomizer bottle and ready your calling position for their arrival. In the other scenario, the deer is coming in from somewhere on the upwind side of you. In that case, just be ready with the bottle. Often, when the deer gets a certain distance from you, he or she will start to veer off and circle your position. Then, you've got to move more slowly and carefully to spray the air without the deer detecting the movement. Woe to the hunter who isn't prepared or moves too quickly. It isn't easy to unearth your atomizer bottle from a backpack or pull it out of the bottom of a pocket when there's a deer at close range.

Using scent and calling together can be a deadly combination for the hunter. Two of their senses are likely to be confused by it. Two of their senses are also going to be curious. At that point, all the deer have to rely on are their eyes. And of those three senses, I'm convinced that they rely on their eyes the least. But that's just my opinion.

I'm convinced that using a combination of sounds can also be effective. In fact, it has been proven already.

Scents will even bring in deer that come in downwind from you.
Michael H. Francis photo.

Rattling antlers for whitetail bucks is a relatively old hunting method. It worked for years and years and years. But in more recent times, hunters have added the use of the grunt call to their rattling sequences and have found that it sweetened the situation for them. By imitating the low-pitched grunt of a whitetail buck, they added more realism to their calling and that resulted in fooling more of the real bucks

Advanced Hunting Strategies ■

that were attracted to the commotion.

In the future, I'm convinced that the addition of the common doe sound and half-distress sound to rattling will produce even better results. It's only logical that it would. After all, rattling antlers is a strategy of the rut. The closer it is to the peak of the rut, the better the rattling works. When a buck fight takes place, it also does more than attract the bucks. It can attract does in search of a buck as well. And during that time of year, it's those receptive does that are the real attraction for the bucks. It's only logical that if you can sound like a receptive doe, you're going to sweeten the calling situation even more.

While I've been talking about scents and sounds strictly in terms of the hunting possibilities that they offer, you shouldn't forget that these tactics work just as well for wildlife photographers and people who just enjoy talking to deer and getting a close look at them.

I've always wondered, in fact, why it was that more wildlife photographers don't arm themselves with these tools. At least, you never hear about a wildlife photographer relying on scents to mask their own smell. To me, that's a frontier worth exploring. Rattling and calling a buck in to you during the rut is also a good opportunity to get some close-range photographs of some truly good bucks. Yet you never hear about photographers packing rattling antlers or deer calls, either.

I'm sure there must be a few wildlife photographers out there who arm themselves with these tools. And, I'll bet, they are some of the best. After all, they've discovered the magic of fooling a deer's senses just as good hunters have. And when you get past those defenses, you've put yourself in some awfully close company with some awfully fine deer.

Rock Rolling and Slingshots

Pieces of the puzzle. That's what hunting is all about. You learn a tactic here. You try something new there. You build your base of knowledge about the animals themselves and what they're likely to do in particular situations. As I said before, the goal of every hunter, or naturalist for that matter, should be to pick up enough pieces of the puzzle in the course of his lifetime to put together a fairly complete picture of the animals they seek.

This commitment to learning about animals has to extend beyond the narrow confines of the hunting season. For those who really dedicate themselves to their sport, it's a commitment that lasts all year long. For deer, that means you walk their trails in summer. You study the mule deer winter range or the whitetails' deer yard during the cold months of the year. And come fall, you dedicate yourself even harder to the task, hopefully learning as much from your mistakes as you do from your successes.

The best hunters I know are the ones who have put in the most time at becoming good hunters. They've read everything they could get their hands on. They've watched every video on the subject. And, most important, they've spent hours and days and weeks and months and years in the field.

Often, it's been the little things that have helped them the most. The small personality traits and tendencies of the deer have played critical roles. Yet the best hunters are able to capitalize on them and turn them into the ingredients of success.

I've also found that hunters who are successful at one species of animal can often translate their skills into success on other species. The good whitetail hunter will probably be a good mule deer hunter, too, once he studies a little bit about the animals. The good bighorn sheep hunter will probably find success on elk the same way.

Perhaps it's because the good hunters are the ones who best understand the animals' needs. They're the ones who are able to get into the very soul of the animals. They know what a new species is going to be looking for. Often, these hunters don't know why or how they know it, they just do. They're the ones who can recognize the trails where game is likely to go. They're the ones who consistently have the pheasants or grouse flush in front of them. They're the ones who can spot the most likely place where a mule deer will be bedded. It all comes back to knowledge, experience and, most of all, time in the field.

Any book would be hard-pressed to pass along all the hunting skills that have been learned over the years. There are just too many of them. Besides, every hunter is an individual. Each hunter has his own style. Each plays a situation just a little differently. Instead, what I hope to do is to provide you with some of the pieces of the puzzle, hope you fit in some more of your own and end up with a little more of that complete picture we were talking about.

We all know, for example, that deer use feeding areas and bedding areas. If you follow the tracks in between, you can get a pretty good idea of the places deer will go and the things they'll do in the course of the day.

But have you ever heard about zone hunting? If you're an experienced hunter, I'm sure you know about zones. But probably you called it something else or just hunted in particular areas without thinking that they might be zones.

Zone hunting has been my description of my mountain hunting for a variety of species including mule deer, bighorn sheep and elk. What it involves is finding the comfort zone for these species. In short, it's the elevation or the type of habitat in which I'm likely to find them. In mountain terms, it's relatively easy to describe.

If there's snow on the ground, for example, you won't find deer in the highest zones because the snow is too deep. The migration may not have forced them to the lowest zones yet, either. Instead, you'll find a zone somewhere in between which holds the majority of the mule deer.

In non-snow situations, you'll also find deer gravitate to certain zones. There might be an elevation that holds a particular type of food, for example. In early fall here, as just one instance, there is a type of mushroom that emerges which acts like a magnet for the deer and elk. For as long as those mushrooms are available, these animals will flock to that zone.

Rolling rocks will often bring mule deer bucks out of hiding.
Jim Hamilton photo.

Once you find the zone, you can increase your chances of locating animals by finding the key ingredients that may be keeping the deer there. The mushrooms would be one example. Another would be a water source. It might be another particular food item. Or, it could be a mineral lick.

As I said, zone hunting seems to fit especially neatly in a mountain hunting scenario. But it can be equally applied to other types, as well. In a hardwood forest, for example, it might be a water course that continues to flow even in dry years. If the acorn crop has been good, there would be reason to hunt areas with extensive tracts of oak. If there's an acorn crop failure, the deer might hunt for a new food source.

The key for the hunter is to find the comfort zone and identify what's making it that way. Then you can tailor your efforts to the zones in which you'll find the most deer. You can work those areas slowly and completely and stand a good chance of taking a big buck that might be holding there.

Another way to make the most of your hunting is to play on the personality traits of the deer themselves. Mule deer and whitetails often operate differently, as we discussed earlier, even though there are other ways in which they're the same.

Mule deer, for example, are notorious for running a distance after being spooked and then turning around to get a better fix on the danger that scared them in the first place. In steep-sided canyons and draws, I've found that to be a fatal flaw for many a big muley.

The way I'd take them is to walk the top of one side of the canyon and to roll rocks down into the timber and brush below. The sound of a rock rolling down one side through the shale, knocking other rocks loose and crashing onto the timber below would often scare the mule deer below. Those deer would invariably run up the other side and then pause to look back down the slope to see what happened. It was during that pause that a rifle hunter could take a long-range shot and get his game.

An old variation on the rock rolling trick was to use our predator calls, blowing them as loud as we could to imitate the wail of an injured deer or some other animal. While the predator call would rarely lure the deer toward us, most often it scared them up the opposite slope, too. Once again, we had a long-range shot.

Today, I'd use the deer call and make distress sounds to produce the same results and probably have as good or even better luck with the tactic.

The thing to remember about rousting deer out of canyons and draws this way is that it usually takes a long shot to connect with the deer once it's jumped. You may have to reach 200 or 300 yards to score on a deer. That means it isn't going to be a great tactic for bowhunters who rarely reach more than fifty yards for a good shot. Also, spooking the deer out of a drainage like that isn't a good tactic if you plan to hunt that area again the following day. In that case, you'll just have to find the deer all over again someplace else. Better to hunt the spot slowly and quietly and keep the deer there.

While rock rolling is an effective method to push mule deer out of cover in a direction you want, Frank Martin found an effective way to bump whitetails in a particular direction. He used a slingshot.

Martin, a wildlife biologist and refuge manager by trade who retired at Lewistown, Montana, knew that whitetails had good memories and wouldn't move in a direction where they had identified danger. So he put that personality trait to use while hunting big and long patches of brush and trees with open fields on each side.

The way he worked it was to go down one side of the dense cover making plenty of human noise. He'd drive his car. He'd walk and talk. Or he'd make other types of sounds that were foreign to the whitetails. If given the choice, he'd make that disturbance on the downhill side of the cover.

Then Frank would sneak back and get on the other side of the cover, uphill if possible. He'd walk slowly and quietly down that side with a slingshot in his hand. With the slingshot, he'd launch marble-size stones high in the air and into

Advanced Hunting Strategies

Whitetail bucks won't go back to a place where they heard danger.
Jim Hamilton photo.

the cover so they'd bounce off trees and brush and fall into the leaves below. The sound of the trees being hit and the rustling of the leaves below in such a random pattern eventually unnerved the whitetails. But rather than run or sneak out of the brush in the direction where they heard human noises before, they'd break into the open in front of him on the quiet side of the cover.

If two hunters are available, one can work the slingshot while the other handles the shooting chores and keeps his eyes peeled for deer movements ahead. For Frank and his son Steve, this tactic was as effective as a deer drive with countless drivers. As a side benefit, it was much safer, too, because only the two hunters were involved and they were always standing side by side.

Both the rock rolling and the slingshot techniques are good examples of ways that hunters took the personality traits of the deer themselves and came up with effective solutions to hunting problems. They're also excellent examples of how just a hunter or two can be as effective as a whole herd of hunters in moving game. Finally, they're good examples of ingenuity and how any thinking hunter can devise effective strategies.

Zones, rolling rocks, predator calls, slingshots. The common thread between them is that the hunters who came up with these systems knew something special about the animals they were seeking. And, they weren't afraid to experiment with something new that just might fail or might succeed in providing them with a new and better way to hunt.

A FEW LAST WORDS

Trophy or Meat or Both

To get the most out of almost anything in life, you've got to have goals and a plan to reach those goals. The same thing is true of your trips into the field after deer, whether you're hunting them or just taking some photographs.

Planning your trips can extend to a lot of different details. Are you going to be out for a day or a week? Would you be better off working close to your vehicle or heading into the backcountry? Are your chances better early in the season or late? And, perhaps most important of all, what exactly are you heading into the field for?

If your answer to that last question is simply that you're going out for deer, you probably haven't done enough planning. It's my firm belief that you should have some kind of goal in place whenever you head into the field. Perhaps, you want nothing short of a bonafide Boone and Crockett or Pope and Young trophy. Maybe you're interested in a good four-by-four, a three-by-three, a two-by-two or a spike. Possibly all you want is meat for the freezer and a fat doe is what you have your heart set on. It doesn't really matter what your goal might be. The important thing is to have one.

The reason for this goal-setting before you head into the field is simple. After the shot is made is no time to be thinking about your goals. By then, your trigger finger has already made the decision. You can't go back. And you shouldn't ever have the feeling that you should.

Too often, guides, outfitters or hunting partners hear someone say that the animal they have on the ground isn't the one they wanted. Often, they complain loud and long about it. The animal on the ground just isn't good enough. That always makes me angry. They simply degrade a fine animal by doing so. They show a lack of self-control, too. And, in truth, I'm always a little afraid to be in the field with someone who would say that they shot something they hadn't intended to shoot. After all, if they truly were careless in their gun-handling or bow-handling and shot something by mistake, what's to keep them from having a similar accident or lack of self-control when a protected animal, livestock or one of their hunting partners is on the business end of one of their weapons.

The solution to all of this is advance planning. If you're going to hold out for a big buck and let the little ones pass, then tell yourself you're going to do it and stick to your plans. If you want to revise your goals as the day, week or hunting season progresses, then revise your goals and be honest about that. And if your goals aren't the same as someone else's, that shouldn't be of your or their concern. After all, these are your goals and you have your reasons for them.

In places where deer are abundant, the seasons are long and a hunter can afford to be choosy, you often hear that does or yearling bucks aren't worth shooting. You have to get a full-headed buck or it's a waste of ammunition and the hunting season.

I can tell you, however, that one of the best hunting memories of my own experiences came when I shot my first

If you want a trophy, make sure it has both antlers in place.
Jim Hamilton photo.

mule deer with a bow. I must have been sixteen or seventeen years old at the time and the deer I took was a doe.

As I think about it now, the shot I made wasn't even that good. I took aim, let loose with an arrow, and then the deer cooperated by moving in just the right direction so that the arrow made a perfect hit. I've made many better shots since then. I've shot trophy class whitetails and mule deer both. But few of the so-called better deer that I've taken have thrilled me as much as that first doe with a bow. I was so proud of it, in fact, that I wood-burned a picture of that doe onto my leather quiver and put a date on it just so that I'd never forget.

A Few Last Words ■

For a young hunter, it doesn't take a big rack to make a trophy.
Frank. R. Martin photo.

Does and small bucks are tailor-made for people who want to put the best possible meat in the freezer and can be especially good for young hunters. I can remember taking my son Wade out and getting him on just such a deer. He was twelve at the time and the mountains can turn out to be an imposing place to hunt for someone that age.

The way I remember it, we started out early in the morning and walked through the timber of the high country for most of the day. Shooting time was growing short when we started walking out down a ridge. It was there that we ran into a little buck with two points on one side and a spike on the other. To an experienced hunter, that buck might not have seemed like much of a trophy. But to a twelve-year-old who had just put in a hard day hiking the high country, it must have appeared to be a world record.

Had I known about the deer call back then, it would have been easy to hold that deer while we got closer. As it was, it became a game of hide-and-seek as we worked our way down the ridge. Finally, Wade was in position for a good shot and he got his deer.

Would you be able to look at the smile on that boy's face and tell him that the buck was anything but perfect? I sure couldn't. Wade couldn't have been prouder of that deer. He couldn't have earned it more. And though he's shot plenty of bucks that were much bigger than that in the years since then, I'm sure he'll never forget the little buck that started it all for him.

Another thing to remember when setting goals for yourself is to determine whether or not your goal is actually attainable. If you're going to hold out for nothing short of a Boone and Crockett or Pope and Young buck, you had better be hunting in an area that has one. Perhaps one percent of a deer population will ever make that trophy status. Many heavily-hunted areas have no record book bucks. And even in the good trophy areas, are you going to be satisfied to end the season without filling your tag just because you never saw the trophy deer you wanted?

Rest assured, there are trophy hunters who feel this way. I know quite a few who go season after season without filling

their deer tags. They pass up bucks that are more than satis-
factory to me. But for them, the bucks just don't fit the goals
they've set for themselves.

To them, waiting for that one buck they want makes it
worth all the time they put in and the deer that they see and
decide to pass on. They have their goals. They do what it
takes to meet them.

For the young hunter, that goal might be a spike or two-
point. For a guy with a big family, putting fifty or seventy-
five pounds of prime doe meat in the freezer might be the
best. Or, there are the trophy hunters who are less interested in bagging the best meat and want the best set of
antlers instead.

The important thing is that they head into the field with a
plan. Their goals are firmly set. And if they follow through
with that plan and keep those goals in mind, they can never
be dissatisfied with the way their deer experience unfolds.

Planning Next Season

Successful trips in the outdoors begin long before the gun
is packed or the camera is loaded with film. It takes planning far ahead of time. In fact, I've always felt the planning
and anticipating provided at least as much fun as the trip
itself.

That's never more true than when you take youngsters
along. Children have a way of charging a trip with a kind of
electricity that most of us run out of by the time we reach
our adulthood. They plan every detail. They dream of
every situation. They pack bags and unpack them and then
pack them again. They worry about details like maps and
flashlights and extra hats and gloves and scarves. Then,
there's the big worry—will there be enough food?

The term youngster applies to anyone between the ages of
two and twenty. Or, if you've got a friend like Art Hobart, I
suppose it applies to someone in their forties, too.

Like the youngsters', Art's anticipating of a hunt begins
much too far ahead of the event itself. If he's looking for-

With a little advance planning, you can have a bountiful harvest.
Mark Henckel photo.

ward to a bowhunt in September, the planning will begin sometime in April or May. If he's got three portable tree stands to place in the woods, he'll build three more, just in case. He'll buy new maps that might be better than the old ones. He'll talk about strategy with people who know the area he's going to hunt. And he'll talk about it with those who don't, too.

As the hunt itself gets closer—perhaps only two months away—he'll begin making his scouting trips to the hunting area. Art will glass from the hilltops. He'll walk the bottoms. If one of his hunting trails into the thickets is grown over, he'll clean it up again. He'll fight the summer mosquitoes, wasps and blackflies.

But by the time the season begins, Art will be ready. His broadheads will be sharp. His compound bow will be tuned. His calls will be adjusted. He'll have practiced bow shots at all ranges from the ground and from the top of his garage, so he'll be ready for tree stand hunting. His mind will be clear about what his hunting area holds in terms of game and how he plans to hunt it.

And, most of all, after all the enjoyment that he had during his period of preparation, he'll enjoy the hunting season that much more.

If anything, Art carries the practice of preparation to the extreme. But he's a good model for many hunters who seem to prepare for a hunt not at all. Aside from purchasing a license ahead of time, there are many hunters who do little more than filling their vehicle with gas the night before.

To be a consistently successful deer hunter, you need to do more than that. If you're hunting in another state, preparations really need to be made up to a year ahead of time. In some states, applications must be obtained and submitted early in the calendar year. If you want to hire a guide or outfitter, they, too, book hunters that far ahead of time. In either case, you'll have to call the wildlife department of the state you plan to hunt to obtain information and the paperwork necessary to hunt there.

If you're planning an in-state hunt, that also will take planning time. Public land should be scouted well ahead of time. If you hunt on private land, you should obtain permission far in advance. There's nothing that slams a farm or ranch gate behind you faster than expecting to hunt the place and asking permission on opening morning. Hunters looking for an in-state spot can get their leads from your own wildlife department, wardens, biologists or sporting

Check the area you plan to hunt to see what kind of deer it produces.
Michael H. Francis photo.

goods dealers. If a city near you has an outdoor recreation show, that's another good source of information where you can talk to guides, chambers of commerce or other tourist bureaus.

Deer hunters with their sights set on a record book mule deer or whitetail would do well to purchase a copy of the Boone and Crockett, Pope and Young or Safari Club International books. These reference works will do more for you than just tell you how big an animal it takes. They also contain information on where trophy animals have been taken and when. In terms of hunting for trophies, nothing succeeds like previous success. Look for the areas that keep showing up again and again in the record books. For one thing, those areas have the genes for big deer. They must also have the food and other habitat needs to produce trophy animals.

Preparations should also extend to the equipment you arm yourself with. Photographers who hope to take high quality slides or prints of mule deer and whitetails shouldn't expect

A Few Last Words

to accomplish that task with cheap cameras and short lenses. It takes a good 35 mm. and high quality lenses no smaller than 200 mm. and more realistically 300 and 400 mm. to get crisp exposures of deer. In the same vein, there are some states where a .22 caliber rifle would be legal, but it's hardly the choice of the conscientious deer hunter.

I've always felt that a .243 caliber rifle was an adequate deer gun. But I wouldn't use anything smaller. Above that, it's a matter of personal preference with a lot of rifle hunters using .257, .270, .280, 7 mm., .30-06 or magnum calibers. Close-range shots in dense cover can be handled well with the old lever action .30-30. If you're hunting out West where the shots can be long ones, go for a flat-shooting caliber in a bolt action with a good telescopic sight. Whether that scope is a straight four-power or a two-by-seven or three-by-nine is a matter of personal preference.

Hunters in shotguns-with-slug-only areas would do well to have their guns fitted with some sort of rear sight. If you buy a special slug barrel, many of them will already be fitted with some sort of dovetail rear sight. If your gun doesn't have a rear sight, it's relatively easy for a gunsmith to drill your receiver to take a peep sight in the rear. Then take your slug gun to the local rifle range before the season and sight it in. With proper sights, you'd be amazed how accurate slugs can be out to about seventy-five yards. Without proper sights, you'd be amazed how inaccurate a shooter can be at even twenty-five yards.

There's no set poundage that a bowhunter should have. In the old days, when recurves were the state of the art, it seemed that almost everyone was shooting a forty-pound or forty-five-pound bow. Today, with high-tech compounds on the scene, a bowhunter has much more latitude in his selection. Because the wheels on the bow make it possible to hold fifty or just thirty-five percent of the peak weight when at full draw, few bowhunters are using less than fifty or fifty-five-pound compounds and some are even shooting eighty and ninety-pound bows. For bowhunters, however, the draw weight isn't the most critical factor. Any bow in that range will do the job. The key ingredient is practice so that they know their yardage limitations and can hit the target at that yardage with the bow they decide to use.

The details of planning could go on and on. Camping equipment, a first-aid kit for your pack, a survival bag with a blanket and food for your vehicle are just some of the extras that will need to be put together.

The keys for all of us heading into the field are to be ready for whatever comes and to be responsible hunters, wildlife photographers or naturalists.

Perhaps now more than at any time in the history of this country, people realize the precious nature of whitetails, mule deer and other wildlife. For those who look into the world of deer with honesty and reason, there are obvious needs for the species to be harvested by hunters in season and to be provided with adequate habitat throughout the year.

Hunters keep deer populations under control and in harmony with that environment. Their license dollars and private donations to wildlife groups help fund habitat projects that benefit deer and other wildlife.

It's a system that has worked well and helped deer populations grow in numbers and spread across the country from the down days of the early part of this century when deer suffered from the stresses of agriculture and industrial development. Those who attack the system of hunting and providing habitat with cries of cruelty to animals do so with emotional appeals that lack scientific basis. They ignore the history of deer in America and the hunting heritage that has helped whitetails and mule deer to flourish today.

Yet to ignore the animal rights people and write them off as a crackpot fringe is to invite disaster. With a population in this country that is increasingly urban and divorced from direct contact with the land, the emotional appeals of deer being endangered by hunters are bearing fruit, even in suburbs of big cities that are crawling with deer.

To combat the anti-hunting sentiment that they spread, hunters are going to have to be even more vigilant in polic-

A Few Last Words

ing their own ranks to weed out the poachers who are little more than wildlife criminals toting guns. They have to support groups like Safari Club International and the National Rifle Association that protect hunters' rights and state wildlife departments that protect critical deer habitat. Hunters also have to make sure that they become efficient and humane predators, knowing that while death is an integral part of providing meat for their families, that the harvesting of that meat is not wanton or wasted.

Planning will help the hunter of today become more proficient. Target practice will make hunters better at delivering a shot on a deer. Calling will help bring the deer closer and help provide a standing target. Studying how to care for the meat of the animal after it has been shot will assure that no part is wasted.

You owe that to yourself as a hunter to become more proficient. You owe it to the deer that might otherwise be wounded by hunters or starve in tough winters. You owe it to the hunting heritage left behind by every good and honest hunter that came before you.

Whitetails and mule deer are precious. They deserve every ounce of energy we have to make ourselves better hunters. They deserve every dollar we can provide for them to make sure they'll always be abundant all across America. We need to plan and make that commitment now. If we wait until the deer are gone or have lost the places they need to live, then it will be too late.

A Little Respect

There once was a time when I figured I knew just about all there was to know about deer. Of course, I was young then.

In those days, I stalked the high country and cruised the lowlands. What I lacked in wisdom, I more than made up for with enthusiasm. I remember making mistakes, missing deer and being frustrated by them. I remember the times when I was sure I had them figured out and they ended up doing something else. I remember, too, laughing to myself about other hunters who I thought were ill-prepared, unknowledgeable or poorly equipped. Those other guys obviously didn't know as much as I did. And I was happy I knew what I did.

I took my share of deer. I patted myself on the back over what a great hunter I was.

I think I've learned a lot since those days. Now, more than anything else, I realize how little I still know.

Perhaps it's because of all the time I've spent in the field over the years that I've come to realize that a hunter's knowledge of deer will never be complete. Even when we figure out the answer to one question about them, that will open the door for two more questions. Answer those and there will be others. Maybe that's what makes deer and all wildlife so fascinating.

I know I've spent a lifetime gaining respect for deer, whitetails and muleys both. I respect them more now than I ever did before.

The breakthrough in the Deer Talk call certainly contributed to that respect. Somehow, when you realize that deer converse with each other, know each other's voices and have some type of common language with other deer species, your respect has to grow. Watching them over the years following the same migratory traditions, walking the same trails each fall and passing their knowledge along to the next generation also contributed to the respect.

It made me think about my own traditions that I was passing along to my own children. I remembered how my sons and I talked. They learned and I learned. Together we enjoyed the richness of the outdoors.

Just as the young deer probably aren't conscious of what they're being taught about the migration trails, I've often wondered about the lessons my own children have picked up. One story that comes to mind concerns my oldest son, Wade, and one of the early hunting trips we made together. There was snow on the ground that day. The going wasn't easy. And I recall that the snow stuck and froze on the bottoms of Wade's pant legs. All day long, as we tried to walk

The best thing we can do is preserve wild deer for our children.
Don Laubach photo.

in on deer, I heard the steady click of those frozen pants legs whenever he made a step. I told him about the need to walk quietly and how to place his feet so he'd walk without a sound. After the day was over, I forgot about it.

It was a number of years later, when Wade stopped home while he was in college, that I found out the lesson had stayed with him long after I'd forgotten it. He told me he had been practicing his walking on campus, just so he'd walk more quietly when he was back in the mountains hunting. He has become a fine hunter partly because of that ability to walk quietly. But it struck me that the lessons of long ago had stuck. Something that I passed off as just a little thing had become a lasting memory for him.

So it goes and so the tradition grows.

Whether we realize it or not, the outdoor experiences we have with our children will shape them for the rest of their lives. The legacy of the land and the wildlife that lives on the land will either be there or be gone for them depending on what we do with it now.

Passing the right stuff along means more than just doing it for our children, too. When I think back about some of the people I've seen in the deer woods and how poorly equipped and unknowledgeable they've been, I realize that they would have been far better served with my kindness and sharing than with the chuckles I had at their expense afterward.

When I talk about successful deer hunting as putting together the pieces of a puzzle, I understand that it's the foundation we receive early on from others combined with the experiences we have ourselves that provides us with those puzzle pieces. Our elders provided them for us. We provide them for our children. And if others aren't as lucky as we are in having good providers, we should do our best to help them along.

In the end that will make all of us better hunters and assure that future generations will benefit from our hunting skills and our ethics.

One other word of caution to pass along is that in passing along this respect for deer and the outdoors, that we can't always force the situation, especially with youngsters. If you plan a trip to the mountains for mule deer or one to the alder swamps for whitetails, you can burn out a youngster quickly if you try to hunt them too hard. Even though they may look like they've got all the energy in the world, young legs are made for sprinting, not the long haul. A young teen might be able to race you to the top of the first mountain and win, but you'll walk that teen into the ground by the end of the day if you keep going hard. Better to tailor your hunting to their physical skills than expect them to live up to your capabilities. Better, too, that you stop to smell the roses along the way than to find you're so intense with your deer hunting that you fail to pass along the other small things about the mountains that you know.

Just as our own love of the outdoors has been nurtured slowly by a life spent in the outdoors, you have to take your time with others. No trophy buck that you charge hard for is worth losing the friendship of your partners. No single deer hunting trip is worth losing the lifelong companionship

Wild deer are magnificent creatures that deserve our utmost respect.
Bob Zellar photo.

that could be developed with your sons and daughters.

Since this is basically a deer calling book, it shouldn't be surprising that I'd extend this advice to helping others learn the joys of talking to whitetails and mule deer. Last fall, one of the high points of an unsuccessful moose hunt was the fact that my nine-year-old son, Matthew, who went along with me, got a chance to play with a deer call. He got to carry his own call in his own pocket and talked to the mule deer whenever we spotted them. Of all parts of the hunting trip, that was the thing he talked about most when we got back home. It was his active participation in the hunt that was most memorable.

The next time we were preparing to head into the out-doors, you shouldn't be surprised that the first thing he made sure to pack was his deer call. And by the time he turns twelve and is able to start deer hunting himself, I'm sure he'll be a seasoned veteran with the call. It certainly wasn't a big thing, letting him work the call on those mule deer. I wasn't even hunting deer at the time. But it made him a part of the hunt. It made him a hunter, too, instead of just an observer. And it made him think about the deer and have a new respect for them because finally they were more than just a creature standing out there. The deer were a liv-ing, breathing part of the outdoors that he was able to com-municate with. The whole experience with the call and the deer planted a little seed that will hopefully be nurtured and grow as the years pass and the little boy grows into a man.

Sharing the fun, passing along the traditions and helping others to gain a little respect for deer and the outdoor world. That's a successful deer trip whether you end up filling your hunting license or taking a prize-winning photograph or not. It's a worthy goal for all of us whenever we go into the out-doors today, tomorrow and always.

Other books available from E.L.K., Inc.

The Elk Hunter
The ultimate source book on elk and elk hunting from past to present, for the beginner and expert alike

Elk Talk
Your guide to finding elk, calling elk, and hunting elk with a rifle, bow, or camera

Elk Tactics
Advanced strategy for hunting and calling elk

The Coyote Hunter
A complete guide to tactics, equipment and techniques for hunting North America's perfect predator

Short in the Saddle
True tales of the outdoors and the funny things that happen along the trail.

For product information, orders, or free catalog, call toll-free E.L.K., Inc. 1-800-272-4355. Visa and MasterCard accepted. Web site: www.elkinc.com Email: info@elkinc.com P.O. Box 85, Gardiner, MT 59030